English Village Architecture

English Village Architecture

R.J. BROWN

ROBERT HALE · LONDON

© R.J. Brown 2004
First published in Great Britain 2004

ISBN 0 7090 6447 0

Robert Hale Limited
Clerkenwell House
Clerkenwell Green
London EC1R 0HT

A catalogue record for this book is available from the British Library

2 4 6 8 10 9 7 5 3 1

Printed by
Kyodo Printing Co (S'pore) Pte Ltd, Singapore

Contents

Illustrations

Preface

This book could have been called *Architecture without Architects*, for the buildings described and illustrated were generally built without the aid of an architect. It does not include castles, stately homes or houses built for the numerous lesser gentry who began to emerge from the sixteenth century onwards, but is about the smaller, less pretentious buildings which make up the majority of our villages and give them their character.

The main aim is to encourage readers to observe and understand the buildings that are to be seen in our villages. Today there is even more pressure on our village buildings with the decline of so many of our village institutions, with the continuing closure of shops, schools and public houses and the decline of the church as the focal point of the village. Yet despite this ever-changing scene there is still much to be seen.

The scope of this book is, by its very nature, wide and I am therefore greatly indebted to all the authors mentioned in the Bibliography who have pointed me in the right direction in finding the more obscure buildings. It must be remembered that, although many of the buildings are either in the public domain or to be seen from the public highway, some are private houses and not open to the public and I would request that their owners' privacy be respected.

Glossary

apse	semicircular or polygonal east end of a church, usually vaulted.
arcade	series of arches supported by columns or piers.
ashlar	masonry of large blocks wrought even on all faces with square edges.
barge-board	a timber board, sometimes carved, fixed at the gable end and following the slope of the roof to mask the ends of the horizontal roof timbers.
base-cruck	a pair of crucks truncated in roof space linked by a tie-beam which supports the superstructure carrying the roof.
batten	a small strip of wood used horizontally to hang or attach tiles, slates, etc.
batter	a brick or masonry wall built with a sloping exposed face.
bond	the regular arrangement of bricks or stones in order to avoid a continuous vertical joint and so increase the strength of the wall.
bressummer	a large horizontal intermediate beam supporting a chimney or floor joists in jettied construction.
brick-nogging	brickwork employed as infilling for half-timbered buildings.
broach spire	a spire starting from a square base then carried into an octagonal section by means of triangular faces.
buttery	a bottle store, a service room for liquid foodstuffs.
catslide roof	a roof having the main slope extending uninterrupted over an extension.

capital	the crowning member of a column or pier.
cladding	a material covering the external face of the building but which is not structural.
clay-lump	clay mixed with water and straw and pressed into wooden moulds to form bats and laid in a similar manner to brickwork.
clerestory	the uppermost storey of the nave of a church above the aisles and pierced with windows.
close-studding	studs set about as closely together as their own width.
cob	a mixture of clay and a binding material such as straw used without moulds or shutters to form a wall.
cross-passage	passage running from front to back of a house usually adjacent to the hall.
crosstrees	the two main horizontal beams crossing one another at the middle and forming the framework of a post mill.
cross-wing	a range at the end of and set at an angle to the main body of the house.
crowntree	the main transverse beam of the body of a post mill pivoting on the top of the main post.
crow-step	projections in the form of steps on the sloping sides of a gable.
cruck	curved timbers used in pairs to form an 'A'-shaped frame supporting the roof independently of the walls.
cupola	a small rounded dome forming roof supported on pillars.
damp-proof course	a horizontal layer of impervious material inserted in a wall to prevent rising damp.
daub	wet clay or mud mixed with chopped straw or cow-hair.
dormer	a window projecting vertically from a sloping roof and having a roof of its own.
dripstone	projecting moulding over doorways or windows to carry off water. Also known as a hood-mould and, when square, as a label.
dutch gable	a gable of curved form crowned by a pediment, characteristic of *c.* 1580–1680.
eaves	the horizontal overhang of a roof projecting beyond the face of the wall.

fascia	a horizontal board to conceal the ends of floor joists in jetty construction or end of rafters etc at roof level.
fenestration	the arrangement of windows on the elevation of the external wall.
finial	decorative termination to a gable, pinnacle, canopy, etc.
flushwork	decorative use of knapped flints in surrounds of dressed stone to form tracery or lettering.
freestone	stone with grain fine enough to be cut freely in any direction.
gable	the triangular area of wall at the end of a double-pitched roof above the eaves line.
galleting	the use of pebbles or chips of stone or flint inserted into the mortar courses – generally for decoration.
hall	in medieval times a large room usually open to the roof and containing a hearth; later also an entrance vestibule.
hammer-beam	one of a pair of cantilevered timber beams which project from opposite walls to support the roof.
herringbone	stones, bricks or tiles laid diagonally and sloping in opposite directions to form a zig zag pattern.
hip	the sloping external intersection of two inclined roof faces.
hood-mould	see dripstone.
jamb	the vertical side of an opening for a door or window in a wall.
jetty	on a timber-framed building the projection of an upper floor beyond the storey below.
joist	one of several horizontal parallel timbers laid between walls or beams to carry flooring.
keystone	the central stone of an arch.
knapped flint	flint cobbles or nodules split across to expose their black interior and used in walls.
kneeler	a corbel stone at the bottom of a gable parapet or coping.
lancet	slender pointed window in Early English churches.
lath	a thin narrow strip of wood used to provide a backing for plaster or render.

lintel	a horizontal timber, stone or concrete beam spanning an opening.
long and short work	quoins consisting of stones placed with long sides alternating vertically and horizontally.
mansard	a roof with two pitches on each side of the ridge, the lower one steeper than the upper.
mathematical tiles	tiles hung or nailed to battens or boarding designed to give the illusion of brickwork with joints bedded and pointed.
mullion	a vertical structural member sub-dividing a window.
oriel window	a projecting window supported on brackets.
outshut	an extension of a building under a lean-to roof.
pantiles	single lapped clay S-shaped roofing tiles that could be laid at a lower pitch than plain tiles.
plinth	projecting base of pier, wall, etc.
portico	roof supported by columns at regular intervals, usually attached as porch to a building.
porticus	an aisle or transept on the north or south side of a church containing a chapel.
quarterbars	diagonal timbers of the substructure of a post mill from the ends of the horizontal crosstrees to the main post.
quoin	dressed stones or distinctive brickwork at the external angle of a wall.
rafter	one of several inclined timbers supporting the roof covering.
random	not laid to course.
rendering	cement or lime-plaster covering to external face of wall.
reveal	the side wall of an opening or recess which is at right angles to the face of the main wall.
roundhouse	a building around the trestle of a post mill protecting the substructure and providing storage.
rubblestone	unsquared and undressed stone.
shaped gable	gable of a curved form, characteristic of *c.* 1620–80.
shuttering	boards between which semi-liquid material can be poured for building a wall.
solar	upper chamber in a medieval dwelling.
staple hall	a warehouse where commodities were stored after

	being charged with export duties.
stud	the vertical member of a timber-framed building between the main posts.
tie-beam	beam forming the base of a roof-truss spanning the space from wall to wall.
tile-hanging	tiles hung on battens to weatherproof external face of a timber-framed building.
tracery	curved patterns in stone or wood at the head of Gothic windows.
trestle	the substructure of a post mill.
truss	braced framework of timbers placed at intervals along the roof to carry the purlins which support the common rafters.
tumbling-in	series of brick triangles set at right angles to the gable to form a straight gable securely bonded to the wall.
tympanum	enclosed space over door between lintel and arch in Norman and Gothic buildings; often filled with sculpture.
underbuilt	a wall added beneath a jetty of timber-framed building to form a flush external face.
wattle	interwoven sticks etc. frequently used as infilling panels in a timber-framed building as a backing for 'daub'.
weatherboarding	external wall covering formed of timber boards, usually fixed horizontally and generally overlapping.
windshaft	the main axle of iron and wood that carries the sails and the brake wheel.
wychert	a mixture of clay and chalk occurring naturally in Buckinghamshire used in construction of walls.

O N E

Regional Village Styles

The English landscape is largely man made; except for the coast and the mountains, its beauty is due in no small way to its long history of cultivation, the pattern of its hedgerows, its fields, its roads and the planting of trees and woodlands. Villages also contribute greatly to the overall picture, all part of the English scene itself, for each has its own individuality, its own history, peculiarities and architectural distinction. Moreover, within each village, each building has a character of its own and, like the landscape in which they stand, the old buildings and other familiar objects which make the village have been fashioned by local craftsmen using local materials, reflecting local traditions. Only in the nineteenth century did this tradition begin to be broken. Prior to this local builders were obliged to use local materials which nature provided; this is the great secret of the English village's charm and individuality, for the local products harmonize best with the face of nature in the district where they are produced.

Geology, therefore, plays no small part in the various styles of village architecture and, for such a small country, England is fortunate in the diversity of the building stone yielded by the various formations. It is the different building materials employed in the construction of our villages that affect their different appearance, for the distinctive regional characteristics are invariably a result of the local material used. Before the coming of the railways and canals building materials were usually obtained from, or as near as possible to, the site, and it seems that the maximum distance for haulage of materials was about 5 miles (8 km). This gives a building a particularly local personality and, in spite of the close similarities in various regions, there is a marked visual contrast between buildings in different geological areas.

Yet it was not only the building materials that dictated the style. The craftsmen in each locality had to learn how to handle and work their particular material in order to produce a sound, stable building. So local builders also had an influence, which accounts, for instance, for the difference between the black-and-white timber-framed buildings of the Welsh border counties and their mellower counterparts in the South-east and eastern England. Climatic and environmental conditions also had a hand; the bleak, exposed nature of some parts of the North and the South-west, the harsh climate and the isolation contributed to the rugged, low-pitched-roofed buildings of these areas, which blend so happily with their surroundings but would undoubtedly look out of place elsewhere in the country. Sometimes a regional style became established by a foreign influence. In those areas along the east and south-east coast which traded with the Continent, Dutch fashions – in both brickwork, in the form of crow-stepped, Dutch and shaped gables, and roofing, in the form of pantiles – are encountered.

Despite the extensive use of 'imported' building materials over the last hundred and fifty years, villages still reflect the character of their underlying geology. It is the diversity of both style and texture and the understanding of our ancestors in exploiting the full potential of the materials available that makes the study of our villages so absorbing. Before studying the village and its various buildings in detail, therefore, we will look at the various regional characteristics.

South-east England: Hampshire, Kent, Surrey, East and West Sussex

The geology of the South-east is complicated and consequently the building types vary considerably. To the casual observer it may seem that brick predominates, especially in Kent, but this is far from the truth.

Timber was the traditional building material over much of the region, particularly in the Weald, which has some of the finest timber-framed buildings in the country; the so-called Wealden houses are outstanding. The early timber-framed buildings were all close-studded, the width of the studs being equal to the space between them. Later, however, as timber became more expensive, the studs began to be placed further and further apart. The spaces between them were filled either with wattle and daub or with brick-nogging. Brick-nogging is used more extensively in Hampshire than elsewhere, sometimes painted as at Micheldever.

1 *Cottages at Micheldever, Hampshire*

There are far more timber-framed buildings than are evident at a casual glance for many have, over the centuries, been clad with tiles, plaster, weatherboarding or brick. Tile-hanging became fashionable in Kent, Surrey and East Sussex towards the end of the seventeenth century. The technique was used in particular to weatherproof the gable ends of buildings and also those elevations exposed to the prevailing weather. In many cases the ground floor jetty was underbuilt in brick with the tile hanging above. At first these tiles were rectangular, similar to roofing tiles, but later, particularly in the nineteenth century, fish-scales and other patterns began to appear, either in the form of bands alternating with plain tiles or in patterns between windows. The mathematical tile was another form of cladding in Kent and East Sussex; here the tiles were designed to imitate brickwork and used to update a timber-framed building to accord with Georgian fashions. Weatherboarding, painted white, is indigenous to Kent and to a lesser extent to neighbouring East Sussex and Surrey. It was not only used to clad old buildings but also, during the nineteenth century, to clad buildings built of imported softwood. Plaster on timber laths was also used to weatherproof buildings but it was not as popular as in East Anglia.

Brick is an important building material in the south-eastern counties. With the depletion of the forests and with little good building stone, brick became the predominant building material over much of the area from the seventeenth century onwards. The clay from the Weald produced some of the finest bricks in the country; the gleaming reds can be seen everywhere. Elsewhere the bricks, although less striking, are also of excellent quality, being various shades of reddish brown. Many walls, particularly in the Weald, have an overall chequer pattern with the use of red stretchers and blue headers. In Kent many of the brick buildings are influenced by the Flemish immigrants who arrived during the seventeenth century. Crow-stepped, Dutch and shaped gables are a feature in the eastern part, as at the house at Little Chart and School Farm, Guilton.

There is little building stone in south-eastern England but in parts of Kent, West Sussex and Surrey, greensand from the Cretaceous system was used. It varies greatly in colour; some are greenish yellow or grey, those in Surrey and Kent are often stained with iron oxide to produce stones of every shade from the palest yellow to the darkest brown. A feature of the buildings built of these stones is the use of chips of stone pressed into the wide mortar joints, a process known as galleting. Another building stone to be found in Kent is Kentish rag, a hard, brittle stone that was difficult to work but was widely used around Maidstone from the Norman period onwards.

The chalk downs spread across central Hampshire into West Sussex and Surrey where they divide into the North and South Downs to surround the Weald. Chalk is our youngest limestone but it is often

2 *Seventeenth-century house at Little Chart, Kent*

3 *School Farm, Guilton, nr Ash, Kent*

too porous to be used. In parts of Hampshire the chalk was not used as masonry but pugged with added water to form 'chalk mud' and poured between shutters. However, around Petersfield the chalk was quarried as clunch and forms the walling of a number of farms, usually with brick dressings. The main importance of chalk is in the flints it yields and, as in all chalk areas, brick and flint are the main walling materials. In Hampshire the flint is often combined with brick to form bands or, less frequently, a chequer-board pattern. Along the coastal areas the buildings are often constructed of flint pebbles, again with brick dressings.

Thatch was originally the traditional material for roofing, but such

4 *Chalk mud cottages at Rockbourne, Hampshire*

was the quality of the clay, particularly in the Weald, that peg tiles replaced it many centuries ago. Thatch is therefore rare in Kent, but it occurs increasingly frequently the further west one goes in the region. Another roofing material found in Sussex and Surrey, south of the North Downs, and also to a lesser extent in the adjoining parts of Kent, around Edenbridge, is Horsham slate, which adds a distinctive character to many old houses and churches in the area. Pantiles, which occur elsewhere in eastern England from Essex to Northumberland, are not a feature in the region. Hipped and half-hipped are the traditional roof shapes in the area especially in the Weald. Those roofed with Horsham slates are generally gabled.

South-west England: Cornwall, Devon, Dorset, Somerset, Wiltshire

~

Apart from brick, which is to be found mainly in east Dorset, east Wiltshire and to a lesser extent the Somerset Levels, and isolated areas of cob, the predominant building material in the South-west is stone. Nowhere in the country is there such a diversity of building stones, from the hard granites and slates of Devon and Cornwall to the fine oolite limestone of the limestone belt, which spreads from Dorset into Somerset and Wiltshire.

The villages of Cornwall, Devon and west Somerset have a ruggedness that is very much in keeping with the landscape. Granite is the traditional material in Cornwall, around Bodmin Moor, in the area encompassed by Falmouth, Helston and Camborne, in the region around St Austell and most of the Land's End peninsular to the southwest of St Ives, and in Devon on and around Dartmoor. Usually older buildings are constructed of moorstone, often incorporating large, roughly dressed stones to openings and quoins. In Cornwall there are other igneous rocks – elvan, polyphant, serpentine and catacleuse occurring locally in the north and east and porphyry in the south. Of these, serpentine, a dark green and red-veined stone found on the Lizard, helps to give this area its own distinct appearance. Elsewhere in Cornwall, much of Devon and north-west Somerset the villages are built of the rough masonry of the stone-slate from the Devonian rocks, or the hard, dark brown-red slates, grits and rubble sandstones of the Culm Measures. The buildings, particularly along the coast, are often covered with coats of whitewash. Around Delabole the houses are often slate-hung.

The New Red Sandstone gives to eastern Devon its fine red soils and also an attractive pinky-red stone. Although widely used in the area there is no village whose character is visually determined by this stone, for it often weathers badly and so is frequently rendered or whitewashed. The New Red Sandstone extends from Devon northwards into central Somerset and onwards to the coast, where the villages around the Quantocks, such as Bishops Lydeard and Crowcombe, are of this stone. As at Crowcombe, however, many of the buildings are colourwashed.

The finest of the building stones in the region come from the oolite limestones. At its finest the oolite provides a soft, dark, cream stone capable of being dressed, as can be seen on both sides of the Somerset-Wiltshire border. Elsewhere the stone takes many forms and colours, from the near white of Portland to the greys of Purbeck, to the light browns and honey greys of the Somerset and Dorset borders and the warm grey of northern Wiltshire.

To the west of the oolite is the Liassic limestone, a less reliable stone which often weathers badly, although it was widely used. The best is obtained at Hamdon Hill, Somerset, which produces the famous Ham Hill stone. This is not only one of our most durable stones but also one of the most attractive: the rich, golden-brown surface is often covered with lichens. Less attractive is the Blue Lias, a whitish-grey stone available in relatively small pieces, which is difficult to dress and gives a rather undignified appearance to some of the villages of Dorset and Somerset, with even courses of horizontal stones, little or no decoration and a profusion of mortar joints.

East of the oolite limestone is a band of greensand: in Somerset, Dorset and Wiltshire this grey and brown stone (rarely is it green) could easily be squared and coursed and even, on occasions, ashlared. In Wiltshire it was often used to form a chequer pattern with flint, a feature which was popular in parts of that county. Greensand also appears to the west of the Liassic limestone, in southern Somerset and western Dorset, from Chard to Lyme Regis, extending into the adjoining parts of eastern Devon. In these areas it was commonly combined with chert or flint, being used mainly for quoins and dressings.

There are many other building stones to be found in south-west England, all of which are used to some extent. One such, which is to be found on the Wiltshire Downs, is sarsen, a cold, grey stone that is so hard it is almost impossible to work. Found on the surface of the ground these stones are of indeterminate size – the stone circle of Avebury and the larger stones of Stonehenge are all sarsen. Many cottages and a few farmhouses are built of this uncompromising stone, sometimes with the front of brick or chalk. In north-east Wiltshire coral rag, a stone that is difficult to saw but very durable and virtually unaffected by climate, was used as rubble lumps laid with plenty of mortar, often in combination with brick. The walls of many of the older buildings have over the centuries been covered with layer upon layer of limewash.

The chalk downs cover much of central Dorset and the eastern half of Wiltshire. Chalk is very variable. It is often too soft and porous for building, but in Dorset and Wiltshire, particularly along the northern escarpment of the Marlborough Downs, it was quite widely used, often combined with other materials. The only area of chalk to the west of the limestone belt is to be found at Beer, Devon, an attractive fishing village on the east Devon coast. The stone, known as Beerstone, has been quarried there since Roman times, but its greatest popularity came in the fifteenth and sixteenth centuries when it was used in the rebuilding or enlargement of many Dorset churches. It continued to be worked until the twentieth century, and can be seen in a number of houses in the main street of Beer.

The chalklands of Dorset and Wiltshire provide, as usual, abundant quantities of flints, which were often used with brick, chalk lumps, stone and even cob. The buildings of the chalklands are characterized by a mixture of materials. Flint and stone is a favourite combination and no doubt a convenient method of making the much more expensive limestone go further. In Wiltshire flint was frequently used with greensand or limestone in a chequer-board pattern, the stone forming the light squares, the flints, which are knapped to expose the dark interior, the black ones. This technique was also used in Dorset, but here the chequer-board is less common than the use of alternative bands of stone and flint. In eastern Dorset, towards the Hampshire border, the flint is often combined with brick, as is common in Hampshire.

A material similar to flint which is found in the region is chert, but whereas flint is dark grey or black beneath the rind, chert is usually brown. It is found in a variety of rocks but usually greensand, and was extensively used around Chard, Somerset, combined with greensand quoins and in Devon in the Colyton-Axminster area. Chert is often found in conjunction with flint, and along the coastal area, from Otterton eastwards to Beer, in conjunction with Beerstone.

Cob was widely used in some areas of south-west England often being preferred to the shales, grits and rubble available locally. Traditionally it was used without the aid of shuttering, producing a wall often 3 feet (90 cm) thick or more; the work was based on the craftsman's eye and innate skill, producing an uneven but attractive wall. Later, in Devon from around 1820, shuttering began to be used, with the cob packed down between boards or hurdles which were removed when the clay was dry. This produced a thinner wall, between

12 and 18 inches (30–45 cm). There are more cob buildings in Devon than in any other county in the country. They are to be found around Dartmoor, particularly to the south and east of Exeter, where the cottages are colourwashed in buffs and cream. To the north of Dartmoor the buildings are of cob or shaley-stone or a combination of the two. Cob is also found in Somerset, particularly to the north of the county around Porlock, Luccombe and Minehead. Surprisingly, it is also found in the Cornwall peninsular, where many of the cottages have stone ground floors with cob above. In the area between Truro and Newquay cob was used extensively in the past.

5 *Cob cottage, Ashton, Devon*

In the chalklands of Wiltshire and Dorset chalk was added to the cob to give it greater strength. Far more of these buildings survive than is generally realized because the walls are always rendered or at least whitewashed, which means that the base is no longer visible.

A feature of Dorset and, to a lesser extent, Wiltshire is the use of cob in boundary walls. The Winterbornes, among other villages, preserve a number of these walls, still on occasions with the capping of thatch with which they were all once provided.

Timber-framing was never a favourite building technique in the South-west. It can be found in a number of towns, for instance Exeter and Totnes, but in rural areas its use was restricted to the occasional porch in Devon and in a few villages of central western Wiltshire, around the Vale of Pewsey, where on occasions houses of cruck construction can be found.

Slate, limestone slates, thatch, and surprisingly pantiles, are the

6 *Cruck cottage, Pewsey, Wiltshire*

principal roofing materials in the region; the use of plain tiles is restricted mainly to the eastern area of Dorset and Wiltshire. From the seventeenth century onwards pantiles were imported into Bridgwater, which later became the centre of production in the South-west, and from where their use spread along the inland waterways into the interior of Somerset and westward into Wiltshire as far as the Vale of Pewsey. Unlike the pantiles of eastern England which are the traditional S shape, here they came in many shapes, the most usual of which were the flute and two rolls, the flute and single roll and the S shape. Because of the nature of these tiles the roofs are gabled, and because the buildings are of two storeys throughout, dormers are rare.

Slate was the traditional roofing material of Cornwall and indeed over much of Devon as well. Unlike Welsh slates, the slates of Devon and Cornwall are laid with diminishing courses – the largest at the eaves and the smallest at the ridge. They are much thicker and heavier than Welsh slates, and one of the unforgettable sights of Cornwall is the wildly dipping and uneven roofs they produce. A feature of many buildings in the exposed parts of Cornwall, particularly along the coast, is the application of a coat of cement slurry over the slates to make the roof watertight against the Atlantic gales.

Along the limestone belt, limestone slates were the traditional roofing material. To the north of the region, in Wiltshire, the Cotswold limestones produce small slates, again carefully graded into diminishing courses. Because they are smaller, they could be used in roofs of intricate shapes, and dormers, secondary gables and swept valleys are frequent features. In contrast, in the extreme south, around Swanage, Corfe Castle and in the Purbeck Hills, the limestone was obtained in large slabs which, because of the weight, had to be laid at a low pitch – unlike the roofs to the north which were often between 45 and 50 degrees. Much simpler roof forms were required, but surprisingly a good many dormers are still to be seen, although these are crude compared with those of the Cotswolds.

Thatch was widely used throughout the region, with the exception of Cornwall. Even here, however, it can be found, particularly in the Lizard peninsula, where it comes as a welcome change from the universal slate. Devon has more thatched buildings than any other county with the possible exception of Suffolk. The houses there – and indeed in Cornwall – are nearly always of two storeys and so dormers are not a feature. The roofs are somewhat plain, with the treatment of the eaves giving the impression of the thatch being thinner than it is. Thatch is also found in southern Somerset, south of the Somerset Levels, in much of Wiltshire, away from the limestone belt, and over much of Dorset. In contrast with the plain thatch of much of the region, the roofs of eastern Dorset are far more opulent, usually with a steep pitch and 'eyebrows' above the half dormers. The thatch sweeps down without a break to cover the porch, and the style is more like those of the New Forest than elsewhere in the South-west.

South Midlands: Bedfordshire, Berkshire, Buckinghamshire, Gloucestershire, Northamptonshire, Oxfordshire

With the exception of the extreme west, beyond the Cotswold escarpment, the western and central parts of this region are dominated by the limestone belt. Stretching up from Wiltshire and Somerset in the south it continues northwards through most of Gloucestershire, the northern parts of Oxfordshire and Buckinghamshire and over much of Northamptonshire.

The limestone of the Cotswolds comes from the Inferior Oolite, so called because it is the lower and older limestone, which tilted upwards at its western edge to form the Cotswold escarpment, some 50 miles (80 km) long, from Dyrham to Dover's Hill near Chipping Campden. Further east it dips under the Great Oolite, the newer rock, which extends across into Oxfordshire. It is from these stones that most of the buildings of the Cotswolds are built. Architecturally it is the most interesting part of the region, for here the quality of the fine-grained honey-coloured stone, which was comparatively easy to work when first quarried, made it possible to provide the refinements to the buildings that are so often seen in the Cotswolds. The abundance of dormers and secondary gables, the well-mullioned windows with their moulded hood-moulds, the four-centred arches above the doors, the parapet gables with their coping stones and ornamental finials, and the ashlared chimney stacks crowned with elaborate cornices, are all characteristics of the

7 Cottages, Snowshill, Gloucestershire

Cotswolds. Within the area roughly triangulated by Burford, Chipping Campden and Painswick are to be found the finest of all the Cotswold stones. All three places, formerly important towns but now no more than large villages, show in their own way the full spectrum of the Cotswold style.

Further north in northern Oxfordshire the architecture changes; here and into Northamptonshire, across the uplands, the building stone comes from the Middle Lias formation, where it is of various shades of brown caused by the presence of iron within the stone. The yellow, brown and orange stones, often referred to as marlstone, provide a marked contrast with the oolite areas to the south and the northern and eastern parts of Northamptonshire. The stones are larger, squarer than those of the oolite, the paler colour of the mortar emphasizing the individual blocks. In those areas where the marlstone and oolite meet the two are often banded to good effect.

8 *Stone cottage, Aynho, Northamptonshire*

Two other limestones from the Jurassic series – coral rag and corn-bash – are also to be found in the region. Coral rag, a stone that is difficult to work and virtually unaffected by the weather, can be found to the south-west of Oxford. Because of the nature of the stone it was laid with plenty of mortar, giving the buildings the appearance of great strength. Cornbash, on the other hand, is an inferior, coarse stone liable to spall and crumble, yet despite these disadvantages it was at one time extensively used in central Oxfordshire, northern Buckinghamshire and along the Bedfordshire, Northamptonshire and Cambridgeshire borders. Because of the soft nature of this stone it was often rendered or roughcast.

To the west of the Cotswold escarpment lies the Severn Valley and the Vale of Gloucester and, beyond the Severn Valley, the Forest of Dean. In the Severn Valley brick, timber and stone buildings are to be found and in that area, owing to the Cotswold escarpment, it is not unusual to find stone and timber in the same building – stone to the ground floor, timber to the upper floor. In the Vale of Gloucester brick, stone and timber are the materials used, usually with plain tiled roofs or occasionally with pantiles. A feature of timber-framed buildings in and around the Vale is the external chimney-stack. Attached to the end

9 *Stanton, Gloucestershire*

gable these stacks built of brick or stone are so large that they appear to dwarf the houses they serve. Timber-framing is again found in the Forest of Dean as well as brown and pink sandstone from the Carboniferous series. The buildings of the Forest are nearly always whitewashed or colourwashed.

To the east of the region brick is the predominant building material. The quality of the brickwork can scarcely be matched anywhere in England. Red is the principal colour, but greys and blues, often used in a chequer pattern with the reds and brown-reds, are to be found all over the Chilterns.

Apart from brick only chalk and timber-framing have made a significant contribution in the eastern side of the region. The best places in which to see chalk, and even here it is somewhat limited, are in the villages and hamlets along the foot of the Berkshire Downs, notably at Uffington where, as elsewhere, it is often used with brick dressings. A harder type of chalk, known as clunch, occurs around Dunstable, the most famous quarry being at Totternhoe. Although it is used in some churches, however, it contributes very little to the villages in the area. Unlike Norfolk and Suffolk, flint walling occurs only spasmodically and there is no village where it has been extensively used.

Timber-framing is to be found particularly in the southern half of Buckinghamshire, the adjacent parts of Oxfordshire and Berkshire and the southern half of Bedfordshire. The framing is usually exposed, with square panels unfilled with brick. Only occasionally is the framework clad and then usually with plaster.

Unbaked earth was also used in some parts of the region, most notably in Buckinghamshire in an area south-west of Aylesbury and extending towards Long Crendon. Here a mixture of chalk and clay, which occurs naturally some 2 feet (60 cm) below the surface of the ground, was used. When mixed with straw and water it had much the same consistency as cob. Known as wychert it was widely used at Haddenham, where nearly all of the older buildings are built of it, and at Dinton. Unbaked earth was also used in Northamptonshire around the Daventry area, but little now remains.

As one would expect, limestone stone slates laid in diminishing courses are the almost universal roofing material of the Cotswolds. Elsewhere, along the limestone belt, stone slates of similar quality are to be found, the most famous being those from the quarry at

10 *Wychert cottage, Haddenham, Buckinghamshire*

Collyweston in the north-east corner of Northamptonshire. Not perhaps as pleasing in appearance as those of the Cotswolds, being larger and more regular in both colour and texture, they had a great advantage in that they could be split into thinner slates, and so weighed about half those of the Cotswolds.

The roofing material over much of the marlstone area of Oxfordshire and Northamptonshire is thatch; the roofs in Northamptonshire are steeply pitched, gabled and without dormers, the houses being of two storeys throughout. As we have seen, plain tiles were the other principal roofing material particularly on the chalklands, although isolated examples of thatch are not uncommon.

11 *Wychert cottages, Dinton, Buckinghamshire*

Eastern England: Cambridgeshire, Essex, Hertfordshire, Norfolk, Suffolk

Apart from the limestone belt, which clips the extreme western corner of Cambridgeshire, these eastern counties are devoid of a good building stone. Chalk is the underlying stone to much of Norfolk and Suffolk, and spreads into the adjoining part of Cambridgeshire. Only in Cambridgeshire, where it was quarried at Eversden, Haslingfield, Barrington, Reach and Burwell and as far north as Isleham, did it yield a good hard stone, known as clunch, which was suitable for building. It was used in Ely Cathedral and in several churches. In domestic architecture its use was restricted to farmhouses, cottages and farm buildings, the majority dating from the seventeenth to the nineteenth centuries. Chalk also appears around Hunstanton, Norfolk, where it was used, because of the lack of other building materials, in many cottages and farm buildings. The chalk in this area was often stained red.

Underlying the chalk in north-west Norfolk is greensand in the form of a dark brown carstone, known locally as gingerbread stone. It was widely used, often in the form of random rubble, but many of the

12 *Clunch cottage, Newton, Cambridgeshire*

estate houses in the villages around Sandringham, have thin brick-like stone, laid in courses with no visible mortar joints, with quoins, jambs and band courses of brick. Such was the scarcity of a good building stone in this area of Norfolk that it is not uncommon to find walls built of a mixture of rubble carstone, red and white chalk, flints and bricks.

The chalk, of course, also provided flints and these are found throughout the area, along the chalklands, combined with brick dressings, in the construction of all types of buildings. Along the Norfolk coast, spreading down into Suffolk, the buildings are of sea-washed flint pebbles picked from the beach, while in the northern and eastern parts of Norfolk they are constructed of cobbles, unbroken flints picked from the fields. Both pebbles and cobbles give a neater appearance than the irregularly shaped flints found further south, particularly in the Brecklands of western Norfolk and north-west Suffolk, where in some instances the flints are roughly halved to expose their dark interiors. Knapped flints (halved and squared) used in conjunction with limestone are sometimes to be found on larger buildings.

Such was the lack of a good building stone over much of the region that even the poorest stones were used, especially in the construction of churches. In Essex and Hertfordshire, puddingstone, an unworkable pebbly conglomerate, is found and septaria, another conglomerate, in the Thames estuary, north-east Essex and along the Suffolk coast as far north as Orford. The conglomerates were used in conjunction with rubble, flint and bricks. In the south and east of Essex Kentish rag is found in a number of church towers.

Needless to say other building materials had to be used. In Essex, Hertfordshire, southern Cambridgeshire and central southern Suffolk timber was the principal building material prior to the seventeenth century. Medieval timber-framed buildings are to be found everywhere, the timbers, where exposed, usually left to weather to a silvery-grey hue. As in the south-eastern counties, many of the buildings were clad in the seventeenth and eighteenth centuries. Here, however, the principal materials were plaster and weatherboarding.

Weatherboarding for domestic buildings is to be found mainly in south-east Essex, where it was traditionally painted black or tarred, although today much is painted white. Weatherboarded cottages can also be found in the south-eastern corner of Hertfordshire. In some instances, around the Hertfordshire-Essex border the black weatherboarding is restricted to the area beneath the ground-floor windows, with plaster above. Throughout much of the region weatherboarding was the traditional material for cladding farm buildings. However, plaster on timber laths fixed to the face of the timber frame is by far the most common technique for cladding houses, and was whitewashed or colourwashed in buffs, creams, yellows and, in Suffolk, pink. The face of the plaster itself was at one time often decorated with pargetting, either incised, with the patterns impressed into the surface of the wet plaster, or raised, with the pattern in relief. Today, because the original plaster has deteriorated, much of the pargetting has been lost, but it can still be seen on a number of buildings, especially in Suffolk. A fine example is Crown House, Newport, Essex.

Some areas lacked both a good building stone and suitable timber, so other materials had to be used. One of these was clay-lump in which clay mixed with water, short straw or grass was formed into large blocks, known as bats, and jointed with puddle-clay mortar. Clay-lump was widely used in central and southern Norfolk, northern and western

13 *Weatherboarded cottages, Tillingham, Essex*

14 *Pargetting, Crown House, Newport, Essex*

Suffolk and into the adjacent parts of Cambridgeshire, Essex and Hertfordshire. Houses were either plastered and colourwashed or clad in brickwork, with farm buildings often tarred. Some of these buildings date from the seventeenth century but many more from the eighteenth century. Clay-lump continued to be used for cottages well into the twentieth century.

Brick was the other building material, and from the seventeenth century onwards it gained in popularity throughout eastern England with the depletion of the woodlands. Now brick buildings can be found virtually everywhere. It has been seen earlier that parts of Essex lacked any building stone and so from the Tudor times bricks were used to construct beautiful church towers, porches, clerestories and even four complete churches. The colours of the bricks vary considerably in different locations depending on the amount of iron within the clay. In

Cambridgeshire and parts of Norfolk and Suffolk the clay from the Gault, which underlies the chalk, produces a yellow brick often called whites. In the Fens bricks of variegated colours – yellows, browns, pinks, greys and reds – were produced, and are often painted. As in Kent, Flemish influences can be seen on many of the brick buildings dating from the seventeenth century, particularly in northern and eastern Norfolk and in eastern Suffolk.

Thatch was the traditional roofing material and the region still has more thatched buildings than any other. Norfolk has no less than fifty-five thatched or partly thatched churches, while Suffolk has nearly twenty. However, much of the thatch has been replaced over the centuries, often with pantiles. Pantiles were first imported into England in the seventeenth century from Holland, but by the early part of the eighteenth century the supply was supplemented by pantiles made in

15 *Clay-lump cottages, Melbourne, Cambridgeshire*

England. They are to be found over much of the region; in Essex and central southern Suffolk their use is almost entirely restricted to cottages and farm buildings but along the Suffolk coast and over much of northern Suffolk and Norfolk, especially northern Norfolk, they are the almost universal roofing material. They are also to be found in Cambridgeshire, where again they are usually confined to cottages and farm buildings. The colour of these tiles is generally reddish-brown but in Cambridgeshire, like the bricks, the tiles are various colours.

Roofs were traditionally gabled. Unlike the medieval houses of the South-east, which have a single hipped roof, those in eastern England are roofed in three separate elements; the cross wings have their roofs at right angles to that of the hall. Because many of the cottages are one and a half storeys, dormers are a popular feature. These were also gabled but those buildings roofed with pantiles often have the roofs of the dormers running down with the slope of the main roof but at a lesser pitch. In parts of Essex and in Cambridgeshire the mansard roof became a feature of cottage construction at the end of the eighteenth century.

West Midlands: Herefordshire, Shropshire, Staffordshire, Warwickshire, Worcestershire

Almost the whole of this region is dominated by red sandstone – Old Red Sandstone to the south-west and New Red Sandstone to the north, south and west. These sandstones are for the main overlain with marls and clays which were, at one time, heavily wooded and which now give rise to the rich dairy farming in the area. Within this general area are isolated hill masses – the Malverns, the Wrekin, the Clee Hills and Wenlock Edge. To the extreme south-east is the limestone belt, to the extreme north-east the Pennines and along the Welsh Marches the older rocks of the Silurian and Ordovician series.

Black and white timber-framed buildings are a well-known feature throughout much of the region, but it is in Herefordshire, and to a lesser extent Worcestershire and the adjoining parts of Shropshire and Warwickshire, that they can be seen to the best effect. In Herefordshire, village after village is built of timber, the timbers almost always exposed and blackened, with the infill panels either wattle and daub or, more commonly, brick painted white. These timber-framed buildings differ considerably from those of eastern England and the South-east, which are of box-frame construction. In the West Midlands they are of post-and-truss construction. Close-studding is not a feature of the region, for here the spaces between the posts are usually divided into squares, and on larger buildings, these squares are sometimes infilled with decorative framing, often in the form of diagonal strutting to form a herringbone pattern. During the second half of the sixteenth century the panels became smaller and squarer, and were filled with a variety of ornamental motifs. Such was the popularity of timber-framing that it is not uncommon to find eighteenth- and nineteenth-century buildings painted to simulate the timber-framed tradition.

16 *Timber-framed cottages, Cropthorne, Worcestershire*

17 *Timber-framed cottage, Hampton Bishop, Herefordshire*

Another feature of the West Midlands is the widespread use of cruck construction in its various forms; Herefordshire has more exposed crucks than any other county. Cruck-built cottages, farmhouses and barns can all be seen and, when exposed, blackened like the other timbers in the region.

Brick buildings are found throughout the region; even in those areas where the houses are predominantly timber-framed, bricks were used for chimney stacks and the infill of the open panels. Worcestershire and Warwickshire are emphatically brick counties and have been so for some two and a half centuries. The brickwork does not display the

18 *Cruck construction, Weobley, Herefordshire*

refinements and virtuosity to be found in the South-east but, none the less, it is often of considerable charm. The colour of the bricks is dark red. In much of Staffordshire, except for the extreme north, and the northern part of Shropshire the buildings are mainly of brick of various colours; dark purple around Stafford, a pale dusty red further east and around Telford a dark brown. However, it is not the colour that makes the greatest impact but the size of the bricks, for they are generally a full 3 inches (7.6 cm) high as opposed to the standard thickness of 2⅝ inches (6.7 cm) found elsewhere. These larger bricks were introduced to counteract the Brick Tax of 1784, which was based on a rate per thousand. The overall appearance is aesthetically less pleasing.

19 *Cottage at Salford Priors, Warwickshire*

As we have seen, the New Red Sandstone covers much of the counties of Worcestershire, Warwickshire and Staffordshire, together with almost all of Shropshire north and east of the Severn. The colour is not always red – it can vary from light grey, often with a greenish tinge, through brownish-red, to a purplish-pink. In all these areas it was the principal building stone, but unfortunately it seldom weathers well, as is evident from the decay seen on many of the churches. However, there are several quarries which did produce a good quality stone; in Staffordshire Hollington, Great Gate and Stanton; and in Shropshire Grinshill, which had a 'red' quarry at the base of the hill behind the village and a 'white' quarry on the hilltop. The stones from this quarry were used extensively, as some of the mellow villages in the northern half of Shropshire bear witness.

20 *Claverley, Shropshire*

The Old Red Sandstone, one of our oldest sandstones, is the principal stone of the southern Marches, covering some four-fifths of Herefordshire, most of south-east Shropshire and the western edge of Worcestershire. Like the New Red Sandstone its colour differs greatly for, although it can be red, it can also be pink, purple, brown, greenish-grey, pure grey and grey with a tinge of pink. The colour may change from block to block or even within a single block. Like the New Red Sandstone, it is only moderately satisfactory for building; sometimes it is of excellent quality but in many areas, particularly in Shropshire around the Clee Hills, it tends to be soft. In Herefordshire, although it was often used for churches and major houses, in domestic buildings it was only generally used for the foundations of a timber-framed building.

An even older sandstone from the Ordovician series is found around Church Stretton and under Wenlock Edge. Also found around the Wenlock Edge and in an area to the west of Ludlow is a limestone from the Silurian series; the limestone is a pale grey whereas the sandstone is mainly brown and buff.

In northern Staffordshire lies the southern extremity of the Pennines: to the east the Coal Measures, in the centre the Millstone Grit and to the east the Carboniferous Limestone. Of the three, the Millstone Grit, known as gritstone, is the most important in the area, for the sandstones from the Coal Measures are usually associated with the industrial areas whereas gritstone is more characteristic of rural areas. It is a hard, uncompromising stone but when quarried is easy to cut and dress, making it particularly suitable for the square surrounds to doors and windows which are a feature to be seen over much of the Pennine gritstone country. To the east of the gritstone is the Carboniferous Limestone of the Peak District. The contrast between the buffs and dark greys of the gritstone and the white limestone of the White Peak is most striking.

To the south-east of the region the limestone belt crosses the counties of Worcestershire and Warwickshire. Except for the Inferior Oolite on the flanks of the Bredon Hills, where the older buildings are built of this honey-coloured stone, the limestone mainly comes from the Lias. It appears in south-east Worcestershire spreading north-east across much of southern and eastern Worcestershire. Blue Lias is the prevailing stone over much of the area; it is more often grey or buff than blue and like the Blue Lias of Somerset was usually obtained in rather small pieces. Along the border with Oxfordshire, on the spur of Edge Hill, the villages are built of a yellow-brown marlstone.

21 *Old stone cottages, Longnor, Staffordshire*

Simple, low-pitched gable sandstone stone slate roofs are the traditional features. The slates are derived from the Old Red Sandstone of Herefordshire, the Silurian and Ordovician rocks of the Welsh borders and, in the north-eastern part of the region, from the Coal Measures. Towards the Welsh border Welsh slate becomes increasingly popular. Elsewhere plain tiles are to be seen; red in Worcestershire and Warwickshire, a dark purple colour in Staffordshire and elsewhere. Thatch was the traditional roofing material for timber-framed buildings of Worcestershire and Warwickshire and can still be found in many of the villages, although much has been replaced with plain tiles over the centuries.

East Midlands: Derbyshire, Leicestershire, Lincolnshire, Nottinghamshire, Rutland

Brick and stone are the two main building materials of the East Midlands. Only in Leicestershire do timber-framed buildings survive in any great numbers and even here there are not nearly as many as in

22 *Mud-and-stud cottage, Thimbleby, Lincolnshire*

23 *Mud cottages, Great Dalby, Leicestershire*

neighbouring Warwickshire. Occasionally a cruck-framed cottage with the frame exposed can still be seen, notably at Rothley and Newtown Linford. Lincolnshire, even from early times, was devoid of good timber suitable for building but a crude form of timber-framed construction, known as mud-and-stud, was widely used and can be described as the traditional building method in the county. Sadly, of the many thousands of houses, cottages, barns and outbuildings built in this way, most have been swept away over the last 150 years or so. Only a few remain at places such as Mareham le Fen, Thimbleby and Somersby.

Before the eighteenth century, mud mixed with gravel, sand and road scrapings, and reinforced with straw, was the commonest building material in Leicestershire, particularly to the south of the county, as well as in Nottinghamshire. Most buildings constructed in this way have now disappeared but a few single-storey cottages have survived, although as these are rendered externally they are not always easy to recognize.

The various rock formations in the region run north and south, from the hard rocks of the Pennines in the west to the limestone hills further east. The northern half of Derbyshire is dominated by two building stones, the uncompromising Millstone Grit and the paler, more pleasing Carboniferous Limestone, often referred to as 'mountain limestone' for it is generally found in the sparsely populated mountainous regions of England. As we have seen, Millstone Grit can easily be cut when first quarried and so the buildings are usually formed of large courses of rectangular stones, all of much the same size, with the door and window surrounds framed by large stones – those on door jambs are often of just two or three pieces. The stone, when quarried, varies from a dark grey to a pale buff colour and only assumes its almost black appearance in areas of high atmospheric pollution. In contrast, the mountain limestone, roughly found within the triangle formed by Ashbourne, Matlock and Buxton, is greyish-white in colour which tends to lighten the whole landscape. The buildings are mostly roughly coursed rubble with the gritstone dressings to quoins and surrounds to doors and windows showing darker and yellower than the walls.

On the extreme western edge of Nottinghamshire, at its boundary with Derbyshire, the land rises to form a ridge of magnesian limestone. Only occasionally does one come across a row of cottages built of this stone, for such was the influence of the coalfields and the associated industrial developments in the eighteenth and nineteenth centuries that brick is to be found almost everywhere.

The limestone belt, which stretches from Dorset to Yorkshire, passes through the centre of this region and yields stone of the highest quality; the oolite from the Inferior Oolite to the east weathers to a creamy grey, the marlstone to the west from the Middle Lias to a rich golden brown. The oolite touches the north-east corner of Leicestershire, extending over much of Rutland and into Lincolnshire, beyond Lincoln to the Humber. Along its length there are such famous quarries as Ketton, Edith Weston, Great Casterton, Clipsham and Ancaster, but local stone was quarried for villages along its entire length. All these quarries provided freestones and rubblestones that were transported all over England from the Middle Ages onwards for use on many of our finest buildings. Locally it was extensively used, the well-coursed grey or whitish stone adding charm to many villages. The warmer-looking marlstone to the west of the oolite was widely used for, although it is less reliable than oolite, it is most attractive and can be seen to good effect in many villages. Much is only rubblestone, for it did not always yield a reliable freestone. Like parts of Northamptonshire a mixture of marlstone and oolite, either in alternate strips of brown and grey or with brown walls and grey quoins, are sometimes to be found.

Further east are the chalk hills of the Lincolnshire Wold; although it produced a hard chalk from the Lower Chalk formation it was not widely used other than for internal walls or rubble-core filling and the occasional farm building, for instance some barns at Elsham. Unlike other areas of chalk in the country the use of flint is virtually non-existent here although it was sometimes used for farm buildings, for example a barn at North Ormsby.

The western boundary of the Wolds is formed almost entirely of greensand. Spilsby sandstone, a greenish stone widely used in the churches of the southern Wolds and also on the contiguous Marches, is not much in evidence in the villages. Further north, however, in the neighbourhood of Tealby and Donington on Bain, not only the churches but cottages and boundary walls are built of a buff sandstone from the greensand.

In and around Charnwood Forest in Leicestershire, is a small area of mainly volcanic rocks of immense age. At Mountsorrel a granite was produced and widely used for setts and kerbstones but it was not widely used for building. There are a few buildings dating from the eighteenth century which are built of large unsquared blocks, but even after the late 1820s, when new methods were introduced for cutting, not much was used. The most important rock to be quarried in and around the forest is slate, the most famous of all being at Swithland. Although stone-slate cottages can be seen in the vicinity it was for the production of roofing slates that Swithland became renowned. By the end of the eighteenth century it was the favourite roofing material, even for cottages, not only in Leicestershire but in the neighbouring parts of Rutland, Nottinghamshire and Derbyshire too. Laid in diminishing courses, their weight was considerable, requiring a substantial roof structure to support them. This weight often caused the roof structure to fail and in Victorian times Welsh slates often replaced them for they were both cheap and light, and required a less robust roof structure. The other source of roofing stone-slates in the region was from across the border in Northamptonshire at Collyweston and Easton on the Hill.

In contrast to these limestone slates, the roof slates in the gritstone and sandstone areas of Derbyshire came from the brownish sandstone strata beneath the gritstone or from a similar formation in the Coal Measures. These slates, sometimes of great size, were laid in diminishing courses, rarely at a greater pitch than 30 degrees.

Outside these various rock formations, brick is today the almost universal material. In Leicestershire brick did not come into vogue, except for important buildings, until the beginning of the eighteenth century. The Lower Lias and the deep red marls of the Trias both yielded the necessary clays to produce good, durable bricks, although not of the aesthetic quality of the South-east. By the end of the eighteenth century many villages had their own brickyards. The clays of Nottinghamshire also produced bricks of good quality. The Dutch influence is much in evidence in the Trent Valley: tumbling-in was commonly employed, while on occasions Dutch and shaped gables are to be found on larger buildings.

Not all brickwork in the area is so pleasing for, unfortunately, in Leicestershire, Nottinghamshire and the southern part of Derbyshire, following the imposition of the Brick Tax in 1784, 3-inch (7.6 cm) thick bricks were introduced which were not as pleasing. Also, by the nineteenth century the tough Carboniferous clays and shales from the coalfields produced bricks which were durable but disagreeable-looking.

Much of the surface of Lincolnshire is of clay of various types and, up until the nineteenth century, almost every village had its own brickworks. Like parts of Nottinghamshire, the county, particularly in the east, came under Flemish influence; tumbling-in, Dutch and shaped gables and other features are all to be found. Most brick houses in Lincolnshire date from the early eighteenth century.

Plain tiles can be found almost everywhere, in particular in the southern half of Derbyshire, where the tiles are dark purplish blue similar to the adjacent part of Staffordshire, but it is the widespread use of the pantiles that has the greatest visual effect. They are to be found throughout Lincolnshire, even in the stone-built houses on the limestone belt, and in much of Northamptonshire and Leicestershire except to the west. The tiles are always red – a strong colour in the south, brighter but paler in the centre and in the north a darker, browner red.

Thatch was the traditional roofing material of Leicestershire and can still be seen almost everywhere, particularly on timber-framed buildings. In Lincolnshire too it was the traditional roofing material, particularly on the mud-and-stud cottages, but although some remain much has disappeared, generally replaced with pantiles.

North-west England: Cheshire, Cumbria, Lancashire, Merseyside

Over much of the North-west only two kinds of building materials are found – brick and stone. Only in Cheshire does timber-framing appear in any quantity; prior to the early part of the seventeenth century the large majority of this county's houses, as well as a number of village churches, were half-timbered, for oaks grew here in profusion. In

24 *Timber-framed cottage, Whitegate, Cheshire*

common with other counties along the Welsh border. Cheshire still has a number of cruck-framed cottages but the majority are of the post-and-truss type, the timbers blackened and the infilling originally of wattle and daub but now invariably brick-nogged, painted white. Humbler buildings have square or nearly square panels, but on the large houses, for which Cheshire and the adjoining part of Greater Manchester are rightly famous, there is a penchant for profoundly ornamented panels.

Cheshire is primarily a brick county, for stone was rarely used for domestic purpose. As elsewhere in the North brick arrived comparatively late in the county, but in Georgian times it became the favourite material even for churches. Although abundant, the clays of Cheshire do not yield bricks which compare visually to those of southern and eastern England. Red sandstone was sometimes used for door and window surrounds, quoins and other dressings. In the flat coastal plain of Lancashire and Merseyside brick was again the predominant building material, often rendered and whitewashed or colourwashed, with the wide rendered window and door surrounds, as well as the quoins, picked out in contrasting colours. In the coal-mining districts most cottages, often seen in terraces, date from the eighteenth and nineteenth centuries.

The principal building stone of the western side of the region is from the New Red Sandstone. In the western part of Cheshire, including most of the Wirral, the building stone comes from the Bunter sandstones and throughout the centre runs an outcrop of sandstone from the Keuper beds which yields stones of various shades of reds, pinks, buffs and greys. Although these sandstones were used in the construction of many of the churches, regrettably they produced a stone that once exposed to the English weather blistered, spalled and crumbled, as is evident today. Locally they were used in the construction of cottages, farm buildings and boundary walls but seldom on houses of any size.

It is in Cumbria that New Red Sandstone can be seen at its best, for it was widely used in the coastal plain around St Bees, in the Vale of Eden and in the Solway Plain. Here the buildings are of large, squarish blocks of dark red stone, with the window and door surrounds painted, usually black but greys, browns and dark greens are also used to good effect. Similarly in many areas the walls are often rendered, with painted stone quoins and window and door surrounds.

25 *Jettied houses, Hawkshead, Cumbria*

Elsewhere, the stones available in the North-west are generally harder and less tractable. To the east of the region, as one approaches the western slopes of the Pennines, the surface rocks are much older and, whether sandstones or limestones, they belong to the Carboniferous series: Millstone Grit, the sandstones from the Coal Measures and further north, from Alston to Gilsland and Bewcastle, Carboniferous Limestone. The oldest of the sandstones belong to the Silurian and Ordovician series. These stones are to be found in the Lake District, where the sombre greys, blacks and browns dominate the architectural scene, often used with random lumps of volcanic rocks or cobbles. Because of the nature of these stones the houses are often roughcast and whitewashed, or often just whitewashed. The outbuildings are nearly always left unpainted.

Much more agreeable is the so-called 'greenstone' from the slate quarries. Around these quarries, such as at Elterwater, green slate was used for lintels and quoins, their huge, irregular shapes contrasting with the green slate-quarried wastes used for the walls. Granite is found around Eskdale and from there to Bootle; the buildings are formed of an attractive pale pink stone, while the field walls are usually grey, contrasting with the slate walling to be found elsewhere. The granite boulders are bedded on a course of thin slates or small stones, which give a striped appearance to the buildings. The quarry at Shap produced large dressed blocks of granite for surrounds to windows and doors. Like the granite houses of Dartmoor, those in the Lake District are often whitewashed.

The other stone found in Cumbria is the distinctive light grey Carboniferous Limestone. It appears from the Ribble Valley northwards and forms a ring to the north of the Lake District. The stone could be dressed for quoins and lintels, but the walls are usually rubblestone and constructed of rather small pieces with a good deal of mortar. Ravenstonedale, in a leafy hollow, is typical. Sometimes the buildings are whitewashed, usually over roughcast to give a still whiter appearance.

Rather strange in an area renowned for its rainfall was the use of mud in the construction of walls. A form of construction known locally as clam-staff and daub was used in the Lancashire Plain. The walls had no frames; the houses were of cruck construction with the walls of clay stiffened by members morticed to a wall-plate and sill-beam and the whole face covered with a thin coat of plaster. In Cumbria, particularly the area around the Solway Firth, mud was once again a popular material, used in conjunction with a cruck frame. Like so many primitive buildings, most have now been lost.

Slates and stone slates are the traditional roofing material over much of the region. In Cheshire stone slates, notably those quarried at Kerridge, are an attractive feature of many of the buildings, including many timber-framed ones. In Lancashire and much of Cumbria the stone flags come from the Coal Measures or the Millstone Grit and were widely used along the Pennines and in other remote hilly districts. In the Lake District slate, until comparatively recently, was the principal roofing material and without doubt some of the most beautiful roofs are to be found in this area, where they are of various colours – greys, greens and blues – and shades.

North-east England: County Durham, Northumberland, Yorkshire

With the exception of the East Riding of Yorkshire much of this region is very well provided with stone suitable for building, the stones mainly coming from the Carboniferous system – the Coal Measures, the Millstone Grit and the Carboniferous Limestones, which also includes certain sandstones particularly those from the Lower Carboniferous Sandstones.

Millstone Grit is to be found on the western side of South and West Yorkshire spreading north-west into North Yorkshire, almost as far north as Richmond, and then intermittently to the south, west and finally north of the Durham-Northumberland coalfields to the sea at Warkworth. In all these areas it has been used for building. In Yorkshire these gritstone buildings differ little from those found elsewhere in the Pennines, but, because the stone could easily be cut when fresh from the quarry some of the larger buildings have refinements. In West Yorkshire, particularly on the eastern slopes of the Pennines above Huddersfield, Holmfirth and Penistone, long rows of mullioned windows can be seen specially constructed to light the workshops. Another particularly prominent feature in West and North Yorkshire is the stone kneeler, which serves as a visual termination of the sloping gable at the eaves. A feature of many of the seventeenth-century farm-houses of West Yorkshire is the elaborate carved, dated and often inscribed door lintels.

The Coal Measures from the somewhat lower ground to the east of the main range of the Pennines, which now coincides with the industrial region of West and South Yorkshire, County Durham and Northumberland, were scenically beautiful until about 1800. In these industrial areas the pollution often turns the stone black, but elsewhere it is usually a dull buff which generally lacks radiance and under grey skies can look a little dour.

The Carboniferous Limestone deposits are far more extensive; they are found over much of the northern Pennines, in the western part of North Yorkshire, spreading over the western parts of County Durham and much of Northumberland until they reach the North Sea above Alnwick. Much of this area is treeless moorland supporting a very sparse population in small villages and hamlets and this stone has therefore only been used on a limited scale for building. It can be seen at Barnard Castle, Middleton-in-Teesdale and Stanhope and other villages in Weardale.

Northumberland is the only county in which the Lower Carboniferous Sandstones have figured prominently for building. The stones are hard, often difficult to work, but the colours – usually warm shades of yellow, buff and honey – are often most pleasing.

The limestone belt continues northward, entering the East Riding at Brough, on the Humber, and crossing the centre of the county to the Derwent Valley. The Lias, to the west, is a continuos belt only a few hundred yards wide and often stained a rich orange-brown, like the older cottages at Howsham, while the oolite is only intermittent, often disappearing beneath the chalk. Only in North Yorkshire does it broaden again to form that beautiful region embracing the Cleveland and Hambleton Hills and the moors and dales behind Pickering, Scarborough and Whitby. Although it contains certain amounts of limestone suitable for building, most of the quarries yield yellow and grey sandstones, which are often of a fine enough texture to be worked as a freestone. The villages built of this stone, most of which were developed in the eighteenth century, are some of the prettiest in the North-east, with their bright red pantiled roofs.

Of the many building stones of the North-east the magnesian lime-stone has been described as 'the aristocrat among them all'. It is found

26 *Stone cottages at Hovingham, North Yorkshire*

along a comparatively narrow band coming up the centre of the region, through the Lower Wharfe villages, then north-north-west, forming the eastern edge of the Vale of York, then into County Durham, close to Darlington, and then onwards to run finally into the sea between Hartlepool and South Shields. Its colour can be attractive, especially when it is creamy-white, and it is seen at its best where the air is comparatively unpolluted, as in the villages of Arksey, Campsall and Darrington.

Compared with the other counties in the region, much of the East Riding has always been short of good building stone. The stone employed for humbler buildings in the eastern part was usually chalk. It proved to be quite a useful material on the Wolds but the only area where it has been used for more than the occasional cottage or barn is to the north of Bridlington in such villages as Bempton, Speeton, and most notably Flamborough, where the walls are sometimes roughly coursed, while some are laid random with brick quoins and dressings.

The flint in the chalk did not attract the builders of the East Riding but in the alluvial plains of Holderness, where at one time humble cottages were built of mud, many of the houses, farm buildings and even the occasional church are built of cobbles – large stones sometimes nearly 1 foot (30 cm) long and 5–6 inches (12–15 cm) across – collected from the Boulder Clay or from the seashore. They produced a wall that required a great deal of mortar with brick quoins, creating an attractive, if somewhat 'busy looking' effect. The material is best seen in the village of Easington.

Undoubtedly timber was, in medieval times, used for humbler buildings but today, except for York and isolated examples elsewhere, timber-framing is not a feature of the North-east. In some areas, notably much of the East Riding, the predominant building material has for centuries been brick. The Hull–Beverley neighbourhood was the first area in England in which brick-making was established as a local industry, with local bricks being made as early as the first half of the fourteenth century for churches and important houses in the area. Local brickwork was often of an excellent quality, with an attractive orange-red colour. Tumbling-in was a feature on the occasional church, such as Reighton, North Yorkshire, as well as humbler buildings. In the Vale of York, apart from the western and eastern margins, brick was also the principal building material, brownish-red in colour. Bricks are also found in South and West Yorkshire and parts of County Durham and Northumberland. Old brickwork is extremely rare in these areas; most dates from the middle of the nineteenth century onwards. These counties do not have the right clays for the manufacture of bricks of high aesthetic quality. As in other coalfield areas, they are mostly made of ground-up shale from the Coal Measures and, although they have considerable strength and durability, they lack any charm.

Over much of the Pennines the traditional roofing material was stone slates, obtained either from the Millstone Grit or the Coal Measures, laid in the traditional way with diminishing courses. Thatch would have been used on medieval buildings, but today little remains. In the remote parts of the County Durham and Northumberland, heather thatch was formerly widely used and was for a long period the favourite roofing material. Welsh slates began to appear in the nineteenth century and soon became the normal material in the coalfields and industrial areas. Plain tiles are also to be found but, in common with other eastern counties, there has been a preference, since the eighteenth century, for pantiles. They are best seen in rural areas, particularly not far from the coast, where it can be said that visually some of the villages owe far more to their richly coloured roofs than to any other single factor. Often along the coast, for instance at Witton le Wear, they crown whitewashed cottage walls.

The Village

It is often suggested that the English village has remained unaltered for centuries, but this perception is in fact far from the truth. Throughout the centuries rural settlements have been constantly developing, reflecting the ever-changing relationship between man and his environment. Each village has a unique history, each telling a different story, which may be due to stagnation, expansion, decline, abandonment or relocation, brought about by pestilence, social and economic change, or sometimes purely local events. This process of change is continuing today; in the last two centuries England has changed from a predominantly rural country, where over three-quarters of the population lived in the country – of which over half worked in agriculture – to one in which well under a quarter live in villages and hamlets and of these only some 2 percent are engaged in agriculture. Indeed the majority earn their living away from the village where they live. The commuter village of today is very different from the village of yesteryear.

There are many thousands of villages in England, varying greatly in size, shape and character. There is no simple or satisfactory way to categorize them, and although there are often similar characteristics each is unique and therefore each must be individually examined if one is fully to understand its present layout. At one time it was thought that most villages, with the exception of those which were obviously for some reason planned, developed naturally, but today the general view is that this is not the case and that their present shape is due in no small part to decisions made over the centuries.

Many villages today were once important centres of trade. Lavenham, in Suffolk, is a prime illustration, a classic example of a textile village. It was virtually rebuilt in the fifteenth and sixteenth centuries from the wealth produced by the woollen industry, in a single architectural style, and was transformed from an obscure rural village in the Middle Ages to the twentieth wealthiest town in England by 1525. Its fame was short-lived, however, as the locally made broadcloth was replaced by other more fashionable cloth manufactured elsewhere. It reverted back largely to agriculture and apart from a few small factories, introduced in the nineteenth century, has remained largely unaltered – a fine example of a medieval textile town. Likewise, Thaxted, in Essex, was once a flourishing town based on cutlers who became established there at the beginning of the fourteenth century and remained until the sixteenth century. When the industry declined fustian weavers and clothiers were introduced to restore the town's prosperity, but these industries also declined and, like Lavenham, Thaxted reverted to agriculture for its main source of income.

Similarly in the Cotswolds, places such as Chipping Campden, Northleach and Burford, were transformed from villages into market towns on the prosperity of the wool industry. During the post-medieval period, however, they failed to develop and stagnated, and today they hover between a small market town and a large village. Blockley, in Gloucestershire, was recorded in the Domesday Book as having several mills and various factories. Later it became a silk town supplying Coventry's ribbon manufacturers and by 1780 had five silk mills along its streams. By 1880 there were six mills employing 600 workers with, in addition, a further 3,000 workers working from their homes, but before the end of the century the whole industry had collapsed and over the last century it has reverted to being a peaceful Cotswold village. It is also hard to imagine such a peaceful backwater as Fordwich in Kent as once the bustling and prosperous port of Canterbury, where the stone from Caen for the Cathedral was unloaded.

Land ownership or tenure is one of the greatest influences on the development of a village, often dictating the areas available for building. It is in those villages that were under the control of a single landowner, that the greatest opportunity existed to restrict either or expand the growth of the village. So two distinct types of village developed: closed and open.

Closed villages were those that were owned by a single landowner who was able to control the development, often building houses in a single style. Open villages, on the other hand, were often under the ownership of many individuals, and became rambling places in various styles, to house the many small farmers, shopkeepers, artisans and labourers who inhabited them. One of the chief attractions for the owner of the closed village was that it enabled him to restrict the number of labourers in the parish and so keeping his liability for the poor to a minimum. In some places depending on the landowner, such buildings as taverns and ale-houses, and even non-conformist chapels, were prohibited.

The siting of a village also influenced its shape. It would originally have been sited in the most convenient position where, of necessity, it required a number of elements in order to survive; the most essential was a good water supply, followed by good arable land on which to grow produce, adequate grazing and sufficient waste land from which to gather fuel. Oddly the supply of good building materials was, it appears, never an important consideration. Sometimes villages were built to take advantage of the spring line sited along the front of an escarpment. Some were sited at a river crossing, at a road junction, in a sheltered valley, or on a knoll of dry land in an otherwise marshy area.

Just as inland villages were built near springs or rivers, fertile land or rich pastures, so coastal villages were sited where fishing was best served by geography. Wherever possible safe harbours were established in quiet coves, at river estuaries with deep water close to shore, or sheltered bays approached through a cleft in steep cliffs. Fishing was never an easy or very profitable way of life but the industry has left behind a legacy of picturesque villages around our coastline, such gems as Clovelly in Devon, Polperro, Mevagissey, Coverack and many others in Cornwall, as well as such places as Robin Hood's Bay and Staithes both in North Yorkshire.

Each village comprised two elements: common lands and buildings, where the whole of the community had rights; and private lands and buildings, where the rights were restricted to the private individual. Most common lands consist of roads, lanes and tracks required for the movement of people and animals around the village and from the village to the fields and pastures. In addition there might be a village green, which might be at the heart of the settlement; and not only would this have common rights, but on it were often sited communal buildings, such as the smithy, the bakehouse, the pinfold, the lock-up

27 *Clovelly, Devon*

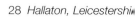

28 *Hallaton, Leicestershire*

and the stocks. In addition to these there were the church and church-yard, the school, any shops, ale-houses and inns. Those elements that were privately owned would have been the manor house, if there was one, and a number of plots normally containing at least one dwelling with its ancillary buildings.

Village plans can be classified into four types; agglomerated or nucleated, street or linear, green and polyfocal or composite. Each of these plans can be further divided into regular or irregular forms.

An agglomerated village is one which has more than one street, with the roads lying at angles to one another, sometimes, but not always, meeting at one point – occasionally with a village cross as at Swinstead, Lincolnshire, and Castle Combe, Wiltshire. There is often no clearly defined shape or discernible plan; the dwellings often appear to have

29 *Swinstead, Lincolnshire*

30 *Castle Combe, Wiltshire*

been placed in a haphazard way, with no relationship to one another and often without a nucleus. This seems, in many cases, to be the result of individuals squatting on the common land.

Linear villages are one of the most commonly found forms, and, as the name suggests, they are usually characterized by rows of houses, cottages and farms along both sides of a single street. Stanton, Gloucestershire, is typical with houses of golden stone and steeply pitched gables on either side of the street, built around 1600. Appleton-le-Moors, in North Yorkshire, is a classic linear village, with the houses and cottages along and facing the street, and the church and manor house at one end. This arrangement, where the village has developed from its original nucleus around the church and manor house, can be seen in many places. The presence of active farms within the street is often common even today, particularly in the highland zone; Thornton Dale, North Yorkshire, is a typical example.

Linear villages take several forms and are often influenced by geological features. They may have developed along one side of a river, where there was little room for lateral development, as at Chelsworth, Suffolk, and Calbourne, Isle of Wight, where at Winkle Street the cottages, each fronted by a bed of flowers, face Caul Bourne; or along a narrow valley where again the room for expansion was restricted. This is particularly true in many parts of the north, west and south-west where level land is only found in valley bottoms. Combe Martin, on the North Devon coast, is typical; it was originally

31 *Luccombe, Somerset*

built a mile or so inland and extended along the valley to the sea. In other cases the landscape forms no such barrier, but the development has been formed along a busy road, like Henley-in-Arden, Warwickshire, and Rockingham, Northamptonshire.

Villages with a central open space, either in the form of a square or village green, can be found throughout England, although in some areas they are more popular than others. They are found predominantly in the lowland zone of eastern England; nearly one-fifth of all the village greens in England occur in the counties of Hertfordshire,

32 *Stanton, Gloucestershire*

33 *Chelsworth, Suffolk*

Buckinghamshire and Essex. They are rarely seen in the highland zone to the west, but are particularly common in the North-east, in and around County Durham.

The origins of the village green are, like so many other things, far from straightforward and there is no single explanation. Some were formed at the time when a village was replanned, like that at Spaldwick in Cambridgeshire. This originated in about 1209 when the Bishop of Lincoln constructed a great palace, built or rebuilt the church and laid out a new planned village at the gates of the palace. Others may have originated as marketplaces or fairgrounds following the granting of a licence or charter to the manor.

Greens come in a variety of shapes and sizes; many are little more than a pocket-handkerchief while others are vast and imposing, like the green at Shipbourne in Kent which extends to some 40 acres (16 ha), and the one at Great Bentley, Essex, some 43 acres (17.4 ha) left to

34 *Winkle Street, Calbourne, Isle of Wight*

the village by a local act in 1815. Triangular greens are perhaps the most common and found throughout England, often where the junction of two or more roads forms a natural meeting place. Finchingfield in Essex has one of the England's classic village greens. In fact it has two, but it is the one near the church that is triangular, with all the classic features, the church, the village inn and the duckpond, with its houses and cottages grouped informally around it. Others are at Cavendish, the most picturesque of Suffolk greens, Long Melford, also in Suffolk, Warmington, Warwickshire, with its spacious green and large pond, and Writtle in Essex. Many greens are irregular – Wisborough Green, West Sussex, is one of the best in southern England – while Nun Monkton, North Yorkshire, is an excellent example of the long but irregular greens characteristic of Yorkshire. Others of note are Pirbright, Surrey, Matching Green, Essex, and South Elmham All Saints, Suffolk.

Sometimes the green has been created by the demolition of the houses in the centre of a village which originally did not have one; this appears to have happened at Quainton in Buckinghamshire, where the remains of the fifteenth-century cross stands at the top of the triangular green beside an ancient track with a large stone for placing coffins while awaiting the priest. In other cases, it seems, the village was built around a large rectangular green for defensive purposes. This is particularly true in the north of England where the greens were used as refuges for animals at times of attack. The greens are completely enclosed by houses, their entrances often at the corners, so that they could easily be blocked by gates, and defended. The village of Milburn, Cumbria, is typical; it has a remarkably regular plan, with the houses

35 *Rockingham, Northamptonshire*

36 *Bolton-by-Bowland, Lancashire*

around a great rectangular green. Piercebridge and Gainford, both in
County Durham, are also typical.

In a large number of cases the village green has been encroached on
over the centuries and in some cases this has resulted in its complete
disappearance. This can be seen at Mareham le Fen in Lincolnshire,
where the green has been completely enclosed by piecemeal encroachment. In other cases the greens survived until the Enclosures Acts,
when they were enclosed along with other areas of common land. In
Suffolk, for example, a number were enclosed and built over between
1750 and 1850. Thus, the Great Green at Thrandeston, which once
covered 50 acres (20 ha), was enclosed in 1857, while that at
Hinderclay vanished in 1819. At Medbourne, Leicestershire, old ironstone cottages used to surround a large open green, but in 1844 it was
divided up and the land allotted to various owners in garden-sized
patches. In some instances the original green has been split up by the

37 *Warmington, Warwickshire*

encroachment of cottages into two or more smaller open spaces. Typical is the green at Barrington in Cambridgeshire which has, over the centuries, become seven or more smaller greens owing to the advancement of the village.

Although village greens are rare in the west side of England, houses were sometimes built around a large open square or rectangle. The plans of Ugborough and of Bradworthy, both in Devon, are good examples and so are those in Herefordshire at Weobley and Pembridge, both with large market squares. Other villages which were built on a thoroughfare have the road widening at or near the centre, which once would have accommodated market stalls and animal pens; Lacock in Wiltshire shows the feature well. Triangular or wedge-shaped market places are equally common, frequently close by the church. Some, like Gamlingay in Cambridgeshire, are large, indicating the medieval importance of the market to the surrounding countryside; others, for instance Nayland in Suffolk, are relatively small.

Many villages are polyfocal in plan, with more than one centre, which reflects their complex growth. Some incorporate two elements to form one composite village, for instance Long Melford in Suffolk, which has a triangular village green approached from the south by a linear development, and Great Bardfield, Essex, with the two foci of the old village well separated. Others have more than one green; Stanford in the Vale, Oxfordshire, for example has two, one called Church Green and the other Upper Green. Goathland in North Yorkshire is built around several greens. Similarly at Romaldkirk, County Durham, the cottages and houses are built around three attractive interlinking village greens which still have stocks and two

38 *Romaldkirk, County Durham*

pumps, one dated 1866. Others have more than one contiguous centre; for instance Hook Norton in Oxfordshire has four adjoining units – Town End, Scotland End, East End and Southrop. There are also some separate villages which originally lay close to one another which have grown together into a single settlement. Many originally consisted of more than one manor, such as Hildersham, Cambridgeshire, which is made up of two manors, and Haselor, Warwickshire, which in 1086 had three separate manors.

Industry was always part of rural life: the blacksmiths', the carpenters' and the wheelwrights' shops and the many cottage industries were present in our villages for centuries, as well as the mining of lead, coal, tin, iron and other minerals, and stone quarrying. Most of these industries were small and located within the village; even the extractive industries were rarely to be found far from their agricultural base. In many cases people working in these industries continued to cultivate their lands at the same time. Other people were agricultural labourers, with their wives and children working in one of the cottage industries.

The weaving industries which developed in East Anglia, the Southeast, the Pennines and the Cotswolds, and many other local industries, flourished. Lace-making was to be found in Somerset around Shepton Mallet, in Devon at Honiton, and in the Bernwood Forest of Buckinghamshire, as well as many areas of Bedfordshire. Hemp and flax were woven and spun into sacks and sheets for domestic use in the Fens; framework knitting flourished in Nottinghamshire and Leicestershire, straw plaiting for making into hats and bonnets in Bedfordshire, button-making (silk buttons in Staffordshire and buttons made from sheep's hair covered with linen in Dorset) and chair-making throughout the Chiltern villages. All these, together with many other local industries, had little influence on the form or outward appearance of the village.

Weavers' cottages, such as those at Kersey, Suffolk, and Arlington Row at Bibury in Gloucestershire, blend in perfectly with their surroundings. The long, curving terrace at Bibury probably originated as a fourteenth-century sheephouse or wool store, being converted to house the weavers in the seventeenth century when Arlington Mill was used for fulling cloth.

Mining communities were often dispersed. In some instances landless squatters established themselves on the edge of the common or waste lands, earning their living both from the land and from the

39 *Arlington Row, Bibury, Gloucestershire*

local mining industries, and creating new unplanned hamlets and villages. In Derbyshire a number of mining villages developed, such as Sheldon, Elton, Flagg and Taddington. Some cling to high, exposed hillside sites surrounded by spoil heaps and disused mines, testifying to several centuries of mining activity in places where farming alone could not have supported a village. Many of the miners' cottages have barns attached to them, indicating their continuing reliance on agriculture.

Not all industrial villages developed in such a haphazard way. At Blanchland, Northumberland, a new village was created by the Earls of Crewe in the mid-eighteenth century for local lead miners on the site of a former Premonstratensian Abbey. Parts of the thirteenth-century abbey church survive as the parish church, while part of the abbey refectory and guest house are incorporated together with trim, buff-coloured stone cottages to form a large L shape square. This moorland village is one of the earliest and best industrial settlements. St Agnes, Cornwall, was, in the eighteenth and nineteenth centuries, the centre of a flourishing tin mining area, as the old workings in the surrounding landscape testify. The old village still retains many of its original miners' cottages and grander mine owners' houses. Of particular interest is the steeply terraced row of eighteenth-century cottages known as Stippy-Stappy.

40 *Blanchland, Northumberland*

41 *Tin miners' cottages, St Agnes, Cornwall*

Until the Industrial Revolution, with the coming of water power to drive machinery, most early inventions were generally designed to benefit cottage industries. Kay's flying shuttle (1733) and Hargreaves's spinning jenny increased the output of home workers without forcing them into factories or mills. Water power changed all this, and a new type of settlement appeared on the rural landscape – the planned industrial village. Communities began to be built around the mills. Cromford in Derbyshire was built by Richard Arkwright to serve his mill on the River Derwent. This carefully planned village is now a conservation area, whose best street is, without doubt, North Street, built between 1771 and 1777 to house the millworkers. The street consists of two rows of three-storeyed gritstone houses with a continuous lintel at roof level, and regularly spaced mullions suggesting that the upper floor once ran the entire length forming a workshop, probably for framework knitting. In 1781–2 Arkwright also established a cotton factory, known as Tutbury Mill, at Rocester, Staffordshire, together with workers' cottages. It was one of the outstanding mill settlements of the Industrial Revolution.

42 *North Street, Cromford, Derbyshire*

Styal, Cheshire, is another early and unusually rural industrial village. It was started in 1784 by Samuel Greg, who in 1799 constructed his house beside the mill. The village was enlarged during the 1820s, with groups of small two-storeyed brick cottages laid out in back-to-back terraces. By 1841 sixty-six cottages had been constructed. A small village school was built around 1820, followed by a chapel in 1823. The whole complex has altered little since the day it was built and was given by Alex Greg to the National Trust in 1939.

Other more modest industrial settlements were also constructed; one was at Barrow Bridge on the north-western outskirts of Bolton, where the village's social, educational and economic life was completely integrated to form a close-knit community. In 1831 Robert Gardner purchased the land and in association with Thomas Bazley proceeded to build two cotton-spinning and doubling mills, as well as providing model dwellings nearby for their workers. Built as back-to-back houses with no back doors, they were considered ideal dwellings, far superior to the average workers' housing of the time. Although an Institute for the community's educational needs, a library and a workers' cooperative shop were provided, however, there was no place of worship or public house. The mills were demolished in 1913 and the village became deserted and the houses derelict. The cottages have now been restored and it is a Conservation Area.

These planned industrial villages reached their zenith in the second half of the nineteenth century. The most famous and most ambitious was Saltaire, West Yorkshire, built by Sir Titus Salt in 1850 and comprising 560 houses grouped around a massive mill. When completed, it had a church, a chapel, a school, a lecture hall, dining rooms, almshouses and a laundry. Industrial villages continued to be built well into the twentieth century: at Stewartby, Bedfordshire, the London Brick Company created a Model Village between 1927 and the 1950s, its workers and pensioners housed beneath the tall chimneys of the brick works. Essex also has one notable estate village, Silver End, which was built for the employees of Crittalls, of metal window fame. It has unusual between-the-wars modern housing: square, flat roofed and originally painted white.

As the tempo of economic development increased, more coal was needed. In those areas where it was to be found existing agricultural villages increased in size to meet the new demands, often changing out of all recognition. Eastwood in Nottinghamshire is one such. By the

1840s new mines were being sunk, which needed new settlements, and so the classic mining village developed. In many cases the collieries were situated at lonely, windswept sites, and around these inauspicious places mining villages grew up. The essence of these villages was cheap housing packed on poor land. Rows of twenty, thirty, forty or more cottages constructed in terraces, at first with only one room but later with two – one up and one down – with a kitchen at the rear and across a yard a lavatory and coalhouse. Backing on to these across an alley was another row. Sometimes they were constructed of sandstone extracted from the shaft but, with the expansion of collieries, machine-made bricks became the preferred material. Yet not all these new rural mining communities were so poorly designed. Houses in Earl Fitzwilliam's village at Elsecar, South Yorkshire, consisted of four rooms and a pantry, a small back court, an ash pit, a pig sty and a large garden some 500 yards (450 metres) long. In addition 'proper conveniences' were attached to every six or seven houses.

As a consequence of industrialization other forms of rural settlement appeared during the eighteenth and nineteenth centuries following the construction of canals, railways and roads. These often by-passed existing villages and so alternative nuclei sprang up around canal locks, railway halts or road junctions. They often started with an inn followed by a few cottages and perhaps a chapel followed by small-scale industries. Shardlow in Derbyshire is a typical example which was transformed from a quiet farming village into an inland port, as was Westport in Somerset, situated at the end of the Westport Canal. Like the canals, turnpike roads sometimes produced minor settlements, or at least led to the change of existing ones; the village of Arrington in Cambridgeshire moved sideways in the eighteenth century to the improved Old North Road, while Cowsfield Gate in Whiteparish, Wiltshire, grew up around a tollhouse when the Salisbury to Romsey road was turnpiked and realigned after 1767.

The new settlements often radically distorted the ancient village plan; villages served by these new forms of transport often prospered, but those that were not often declined. Later, with the concentration of manufacturing industries in the towns, industries that were at one time widespread in the countryside began to be relocated in those areas of high urban population. In many instances industrial villages developed into large towns; many of the industrial towns of northern Staffordshire were originally poor villages relying on subsistence agriculture which began to prosper in the seventeenth century with the introduction of pottery and coal mining.

Although many villages appear to have been built with little or no planning there are some which were obviously planned. In medieval times, between around 900 to 1200, many villages were deliberately created or replanned all over England. This was often done by local lords and formed the approach to the gateway to a castle or monastery, or the gatehouse of a large house (Kimbolton, Cambridgeshire, and Portchester, Hampshire) or placed around a green or square to the front of these buildings (the ancient village of Blanchland, Northumberland, and the villages of Muchelney, Somerset, and Chilham, Kent). However, most date from the late sixteenth and early seventeenth centuries, the period of great rebuilding, when the old, flimsily constructed buildings of the medieval period were swept away to be replaced by more substantial buildings in what W.G. Hoskins has termed the 'rebuilding of rural England'. Most of the old buildings seen in our villages today date from this period, with the exception of Cumbria, Northumberland and County Durham, where much of the rebuilding dates from after 1690. This great rebuilding saw not only the construction of new dwellings but also a wide range of public buildings. The process continued throughout the eighteenth century and there can hardly be a village that has not been affected.

Some were affected more than others. While the medieval lord of the manor was content to have his house within the village, his successor was often keen to distance himself from this tenants and either built his new dwelling away from their cottages or, on occasions destroyed the village and rebuilt it out of his view – a process known as emparking.

At first it was not uncommon for the village to be totally destroyed without any attempt to rehouse the tenants. Fawsley in Northampton is one good early example of this; the Knightly family, who had acquired the estate early in the fifteenth century, had, by the end of the century, evicted all the tenants in order to build a fine Tudor mansion in a parkland setting, with no attempt to recreate the village. Similarly at Great Sandon, in Staffordshire, the Erdeswicke family, who owned the manor, destroyed the village and emparked the site in about 1600, the ousted villagers having to settle in the nearby village of Little Sandon (now Sandon). During the seventeenth and eighteenth centuries, however, a greater effort was made to rehouse at least some of the tenants, although often, when emparking involved the enclosure of arable land, many must have been forced to leave.

Although there are examples of new villages in the seventeenth century – Sudbury in Derbyshire and the original estate of Great Tew in Oxfordshire – it was the eighteenth century that was the great age of emparking. At first these new villages were often characterized by houses of uniform size and design placed in rows, often on the approaches to the new mansion. One of the first examples was at Chippenham in Cambridgeshire, where Edward Russell, First Lord of the Admiralty and later Lord Orford, bought up some 500 acres (200 ha) from five landowners at the end of the seventeenth century. By 1712 the new park and artificial lake had engulfed half the village. A new village was built, consisting of fifty single-storey semi-detached cottages, each pair linked by outbuildings. In addition a charity school and church were built. In about 1729 Sir Robert Walpole constructed a new village outside the gates of his new mansion, Houghton Hall in Norfolk. The new village (New Houghton) consisted of two rows of whitewashed brick and pantiled cottages. In addition to these twenty-five dwellings, contained in ten buildings, Sir Robert also constructed some single-storey almshouses and two farmhouses.

43 *Chippenham, Cambridgeshire*

Perhaps the most celebrated example of emparking is to be found at Nuneham Courtenay in Oxfordshire. The village was built in 1761 by Lord Harcourt to replace the old village which stood behind his newly built Palladian mansion. The cottages, like those at New Houghton, were placed at intervals on either side of the road, but rather than on the approach road to the park, along the main Oxford to London road. The cottages, all identical and semi-detached, were constructed of brick with timber-framed gable ends. The church, like so many examples of emparking, was retained within the park but in this instance it was demolished to be replaced as a classical temple to complement the landscape design.

At Milton Abbas in Dorset, following the destruction of a sizeable market town (which included a grammar school, almshouses, shops, four inns and a brewery), two rows of forty identical cottages were built, broken only by the church and almshouses. The work was carried out for Joseph Damer, later Earl of Dorchester, probably by William Chambers, who had been employed to carry out extensive alterations to Milton Abbey. The village was commenced in 1773 and not completed until fifteen years later. Each cottage had four rooms – two downstairs and two upstairs – entered through a common front door. Between each pair of cottages was planted a horse-chestnut tree to soften the repetitive arrangement. Today it has become a fashionable commuter and retirement village; the cottages, which at one time housed four families in each semi-detached pair, have generally been renovated but still retain their original appearance.

Towards the end of the eighteenth century the Picturesque movement began to gain momentum and many of the earlier planned villages were criticised, particularly Nuneham Courtenay which was described as 'too like rows of street houses'. From around 1790 designs for Picturesque cottages appeared constantly in pattern books. At first these books showed cottages which were basically symmetrical, with the ornamental detail simply added, but later they became more florid and even more irregular. Many isolated romantic cottages built in the Picturesque style and adapted to the park scenery of the great estates began to be built at the beginning of the nineteenth century, and in 1810 the first complete Picturesque village was built for John Scandrett Harford, a Quaker banker, at Blaise Hamlet, Henbury, near Bristol, to house his retired servants. The village, with its nine cottages – eight single and one double – dispersed about an

44 *Milton Abbas, Dorset*

undulating, curving central village green with a pump-cum-sundial and weathervane as its focal point, was designed by John Nash. Each cottage differs in style from its neighbours with little regard for local building styles. They are stone-built, some with stone slate roofs, some thatched with enormous projections over the windows and all with ornamental brick chimneys of considerable size. The group is now owned by the National Trust.

Blaise Hamlet became the model for subsequent Picturesque villages and an important port of call for all those interested in the movement. Other Picturesque villages followed; Sir Thomas Dyke Acland built the village of Selworthy in Somerset in 1828 as a place of retirement for his estate pensioners. Although he employed no architect he was obviously influenced by Nash's village of Blaise Hamlet. The seven pretty cream-washed thatched cottages are loosely grouped

45 *Blaise Hamlet, near Bristol*

46 *Selworthy, Somerset*

around a sloping green at the foot of a steep wooded combe climbing to Selworthy Beacon. Unlike Blaise Hamlet they are built to incorporate almost all the features to be seen locally – the tall chimneys (some of them circular), the projecting ovens and the deep thatched eaves and eyebrow dormers – but all given some Picturesque feature.

On a much grander scale is the village of Edensor in Derbyshire built in 1838 after the 6th Duke of Devonshire visited Blaise Hamlet in 1835 with his gardener Joseph Paxton (who later went on to design the Crystal Palace). Paxton laid out the village, but the houses and cottages were designed by John Robertson, who had been J.C. Loundon's draughtsman. No two buildings are alike and in a riot of architectural fancy Robertson gave them Swiss chalet roofs, Italian-style windows,

47 *Edensor, Derbyshire*

Jacobean gables, Tudor chimneys and Georgian doorways. Paxton made sure the houses were placed well apart, surrounding a broad green planted with laburnum trees.

Another village, said to be influenced by Blaise Hamlet, is Somerleyton in Suffolk, which was built by Sir Samuel Morton Peto, who made his fortune from railway construction. In around 1850 he built, at the gates of his great mansion Somerleyton Hall, twenty-eight cottages placed around a great open, square green with an iron pump of 1857, a few carefully planted trees and a school building. It is probably the most successful of the Picturesque villages. The school is mock-Tudor and some of the cottages are thatched, with rendered and brick walls with false timber-framing in bizarre patterns.

Littlebredy, Dorset, is another essay in Picturesque estate housing which owes much to Blaise Hamlet, but it is more complex and diffuse. The cottages are grouped around a rough, irregular green at the top, with a magnificent contrived view from it to the west down the Bride Valley.

At Old Warden, Bedfordshire, Lord Ongley improved his village around the middle of the nineteenth century. He not only incorporated Picturesque details, such as intricate thatched roofs with deep projecting eaves, elaborate barge-boards, lattice-work porches and fanciful casement

48 *Somerleyton, Suffolk*

windows in his cottages, but also made subtle use of the landscape, as well as planting evergreen trees and bushes to add to the overall effect. Murray's *Guide to Hertfordshire, Bedfordshire and Buckinghamshire,* published in 1895, describes it thus:

> The quaint houses with curved barge-boards and red painted doors and windows and covered with ivy and honeysuckle and all Picturesque, were for the most part devised and arranged by Lord Ongley in whose time Old Warden was one of the sights of Bedfordshire – the inhabitants, by aid of red cloaks and tall hats being made to harmonise with their dwellings.

In some instances landowners, instead of rebuilding their villages, retained many of their older cottages, adding Picturesque detailing and sometimes providing additional cottages built in the same idiom to complete the effect. One such village is Harlaxton in Lincolnshire, which was partially rebuilt and heavily restored in the Picturesque style by Anthony Salvin for George de Ligne Gregory.

The cottages at Stisted, Essex, were also given heavy Picturesque detailing when the landlord Onley Savil Onley restored them in the middle of the nineteenth century. He was assisted by a builder named Watts whose passion, it seems, was mock-Tudor chimneys, something for which Stisted is now well-known. A close inspection reveals the date of erection and the initials OSO for Onley Savil Onley or JSO for his wife, Jane Savil Onley. A village school and a working men's club were also built at this time.

Another example is Great Tew in Oxfordshire, where the original estate village, built in the middle of the seventeenth century by Lucius Carey, Viscount Falkland, was renovated with the addition of Picturesque details, such as rustic porches, and much of its charm is due to the careful planting of trees, probably by John Loundon, who was farm steward to Colonel G.F. Stratton between 1809 and 1811. Matthew Robinson Boulton was responsible for further embellishing and rebuilding many of the cottages, as well as the new link road to the Square. The eighteenth-century Falkland Arms looks across to the gabled school with an adjoining teacher's house built by his son.

Influenced by the Arts and Crafts movement, which gained momentum at the end of the nineteenth century, and to combat the

49 *Falkland Arms, Great Tew, Oxfordshire*

uniform ugliness of industrial housing, Picturesque villages continued to be built well into the first part of the twentieth century. In 1900 the Hon. Charles Rothschild undertook the construction of the village of Ashton, Northamptonshire. Huckvale, an architect employed by the Rothschilds on their estates in Buckinghamshire and Hertfordshire, undertook the work in the Picturesque idiom, with stone thatched cottages clustering around the village green.

Edwin Lutyens was among the foremost Arts and Crafts architects of his day, and although he never built a complete village, he was often commissioned to build cottages for labourers, the most notable being the row of cottages for the Hon. Ivor Guest at Ashby St Ledgers, Northamptonshire. When built each cottage boasted a kitchen, a

50 *Ashby St Ledgers, Northamptonshrie*

scullery, a parlour and three bedrooms. The hamlet of Bladen Valley, to the west of Sir Ernest Debenham's estate village of Briantspuddle in Dorset is an imitation of Blaise Hamlet. Building commenced in 1914 to the design of Halsey Ricardo, a leading figure in Arts and Crafts architecture, and Macdonald Gill. The thatched and whitewashed cottages were built around a large war memorial undertaken by Macdonald Gill's brother Eric in 1916–18. Ricardo and Gill had already been commissioned by Sir Ernest to build the estate village at Briantspuddle.

Ardeley, Hertfordshire, which was designed by F.C. Eden in 1917, is another twentieth-century example; the white-painted thatched cottages and thatched village hall are built around the village green, with its brick pumphouse. This village is also based upon Blaise Hamlet, but without the capriciousness of the original.

The process of emparking and the creation of estate villages continued well into the nineteenth century. Many are found within a day's coach ride from London, particularly on the borders of Northamptonshire, Buckinghamshire and Oxfordshire. The most ambitious is the one created at Waddesdon, Buckinghamshire, by Baron Ferdinand de Rothschild, who bought the land in 1874. Almost everything in the village was built by the Rothschilds; all the cottages are half-timbered, although they date from 1880 to probably the early twentieth century. In addition to the houses and cottages, a club and a reading room were built in 1883 and in the same year the almshouses, although they were originally founded in 1646, and the school. Later, in 1887, came a hotel and in 1889 the village hall. These buildings were all built in a dark red brick. All carry the Rothschild emblem of five arrows.

Many landowners found villages built in the Picturesque style expensive both to build and to maintain, and many model and estate villages were built in a more traditional style. There are numerous examples of eighteenth- and nineteenth-century estate villages throughout England. Many are characterized by straight roads with houses of similar dimensions, usually semi-detached or terraced, built in a simple style. This happened at Mixbury in Oxfordshire, a village of semi-detached brick cottages built along the road leading from the church to the earthworks of Beaumont Castle. It was created on the orders of the Court of Chancery in the late nineteenth century. The larger estates provided good housing, in particular those owned by the Duke of Bedford at Husborne Crawley, Lidlington, Ridgmont, Willington and Woburn, all in Bedfordshire, as well as those at Chenies, Buckinghamshire. These red-brick gabled houses date mainly from the early to mid-nineteenth century (except for Woburn which is mostly eighteenth-century).

Other landowners built in a similar style; Ripley, North Yorkshire, at the lower end of Nidderdale, is a prime example built by Sir William Amcotts Ingilby (whose family has been at Ripley since about 1350) to replace the old thatched cottages. The sturdy terraces of two-storey gritstone cottages, with Tudor-Gothic detailing, are built along both sides of the road running at right angles to a triangular 'square' in which the large ornate Church of All Saints, the market cross and stocks make an important focal point. The work was commenced in 1827 and was not completed until 1860. Overpowering the unassuming rows of terraces is the flamboyant Hotel de Ville, a Gothic creation dated 1854, complete with battlements and large mullioned windows. Sir William died before completion but the work was finished by his widow. The building is now the village hall and post office. There is also a school of 1831 built in the form of a chapel.

Many estate villages are not of one build, nor by one owner. Cambo, Northumberland, is very much an estate village. The building started in 1730 under Sir Walter Blackett, and continued for almost two centuries under successive owners of the Wallington estates. The

51 *Cambo, Northumberland*

most notable addition was North Row, a group of late-nineteenth-century gabled houses overlooking the village green built by Sir Charles Trevelyan.

Churches and Chapels

Village Churches

Many people's idea of an English village centres around the church, with its tower, possibly with a spire, rising above the village, with humble cottages and houses clustered around it for protection. In most cases the church will be the oldest building in the village, and will have been a comforting sight for countless generations over the centuries, serving not only as a place of worship but also as the centre of social and even business activities and assuming an importance in the lives of the villagers that no building can have today. Generation after generation of families have, in the past been baptized, married and buried at the village church. After the Dissolution of the Monasteries churches became the centres for raising charitable alms for the poor of the parish. The nave, which belonged to the laity and was uncluttered by pews, was, up until 1571, used for parish meetings as well as feasting and entertainment on saints' days and holidays, a procedure known as church-ales.

Throughout the centuries village churches have seen – and suffered the effects of – many changes; they may have lost some of their valuables during the Reformation, seen their wall paintings obliterated, had priceless sculptures, wood carvings and stained glass destroyed by the Puritans as too idolatrous, and suffered almost as much destruction at the hands of Victorians, with their over-zealous restoration. Yet they have remained the village centre and although they are today maintained and attended by an ever-dwindling congregation, a village without its church is inconceivable and its days are far from numbered, for it still holds together the village fabric and still remains its focal point.

The size and grandeur of many of our village churches reflect the prosperity of the village and its surrounding countryside. The size of a church bears no true relationship to the size of the village, either now or in the past, for it generally reflected the wealth and devotion of its patron. This might be a wealthy individual or a group of people, such as a guild. Their motives were no doubt mixed, for although the church was undoubtedly built to the glory of God it was also often built to the vanity of man. The magnificent 'wool' churches built during the fifteenth century in the Cotswolds, East Anglia and other parts of eastern England reflect the great wealth of the wool trade and cloth manufacture in these areas. In other areas, where land was poor – in particular the upland areas of England – the parishes were larger but the villages were smaller and this was often reflected in their churches, which were often only of two cells, nave and chance, with a bell-cot instead of a tower.

Although the normal location for the church is the key central position within the heart of the community, there are many which are situated away from the village. The reason for their isolation is not always clear and may reflect the desertion of the original village because of plague, war, economic or social factors or repeated crop failure. For whatever reason these isolated churches are often the least spoilt, but also, as they no longer perform any useful function, the most vulnerable. Others stand remote from any habitation except a single house – the classic English ensemble of church and manor house which dates back to the time when the lord of the manor was responsible for the construction of the village church, which frequently led to its siting close to his house. In later years many manor houses became farmhouses and their churches today are surrounded by farm buildings, often approached along a private road or track. In other cases the old manor house was enlarged or rebuilt to become the 'big' house, with the medieval church often close by or forming the focal point of a landscaped park. In still other instances the medieval church was demolished and replaced with one built in the Gothick (not to be confused with the later Gothic revival) or the neo-Classical style so popular with the landed gentry in the eighteenth century.

Christianity arrived in England during Roman times, but it was largely suppressed by the pagan Saxons over much of England. Their conversion began at the end of the sixth century with the arrival of St Augustine's mission in Kent in 597 and a study of English churches effectively begins at this time. In the north, church-building arrived in Northumbria in 674 when Benedict Biscop, a French monk of noble birth, brought stonemasons from Gaul to construct his monasteries at Monkwearmouth and Jarrow. The original parts of these two churches still remain.

Early surviving Saxon churches in the south are based on the Roman basilica but little survives of them to give us a picture of what they looked like. One of which substantial remains do survive, and which can be accurately dated, is St Peter's, Bradwell-on-Sea, Essex, founded by St Cedd in 654. All that now remains is the nave (the apsed chancel, west porch, and north and south porticus have all disappeared).

A far more ambitious church, based on the same lines, is All Saints, Brixworth, Northamptonshire. It is without doubt the outstanding church of its period in England, having been built some two or three hundred years after the Romans left Britain. The present church is now smaller than it was originally. What have survived are the nave, presbytery, the central section of the tower and the sunken ambulatory round the apse. The apse itself was rebuilt on the old foundation in 1865. The main west entrance doorway, the two porches on either side of the central porch of the tower, the side compartments to the nave (known as the porticus), and the original apse with possibly a chapel below have all disappeared. In place of the west doorway a stair turret was added, possibly in the tenth century. A lady chapel was built in the thirteenth century and the broach spire in about 1350. The church has been described by Sir Alfred Clapham as 'perhaps the most imposing architectural memorial of the seventh century surviving north of the Alps'.

However, these early stone Saxon churches would not have been typical. Most would have been constructed of timber, but not much is known about these. Many were probably replaced by stone before the Norman conquest, and this is borne out at Wharram Percey, North Yorkshire, where excavations have revealed that an original single-celled timber church was replaced by a single-celled church of stone, then by a two-celled church and again by a much larger two-celled church, all within the Saxon period. The only surviving example of Saxon timber building is at Greensted-Juxta-Ongar, in Essex, built, it is believed, as early as the beginning of the eleventh century. The nave walls are of split oak logs (staves) set vertically and jointed together by oak tongues let into grooves. Originally the timbers would have been set in the ground but in the sixteenth century, when the ends had decayed, a timber sill was introduced. The present brick plinth and oak sill date from the restoration in 1852, when decay to the staves resulted in their further reduction. Excavations have revealed traces of two former chancels with timber walls. Traditionally the church is where St Edmund's body rested on its way from London to Bury St Edmunds in 1013.

By the end of the seventh century two distinct stone types had developed: the Augustinian or Kentish church, which in proportion was about twice as long as it was wide, with an apsed sanctuary and often a right and left porticus; and the Northumberland church, which was about three times as long as it was wide with a minute square sanctuary, reflecting Celtic rather than Roman traditions. Both are lofty; the height of the Northumberland type is exaggerated by its narrowness. From these two schools of building the characteristic English church was to emerge. Although some of the larger churches had porticus and even occasionally aisles, as at Wing, Buckinghamshire, and Great Paxton, Cambridgeshire, the majority were either a single cell, without a separate sanctuary, or a nave-and-chancel church.

There are some 250 village churches with substantial Saxon remains and even a few which are more or less complete Saxon buildings. The most remarkable is perhaps the one at Escombe, County Durham, built in the seventh century reusing Roman material, which has remained virtually intact. Its tall, narrow nave and very small square chancel must have been typical of many of the early churches in northern England. The south side has been altered by the addition of a porch and the insertion of lancet windows to give much-needed light but the north side shows how austere these early churches were. The chancel is only 10 feet (3 metres) square and it is possible that there was originally no east window. The chancel arch is tall and narrow. The crow-stepped gable and slates are not original; what the original roof covering was is now unknown.

There is a much larger Saxon church, built in the late tenth century, at Breamore, Hampshire. It is cruciform, and has little altered over the centuries. The chancel has been rebuilt but is so small that the new one was probably built on the original foundations. The south porch is a later

52 *Saxon church, Breamore, Hampshire*

addition and only a few of the original windows still survive, but the walling and therefore its proportions remain basically Saxon. The central tower, which rises only just above the nave roof, is capped by a later square turret which must have replaced an earlier roof of similar design.

A few churches still have Saxon towers; early ones were raised above their existing two-storeyed west porches, such as at Corbridge, Northumberland, and at Brixworth and Brigstock, both in Northamptonshire. Later towers of exceptional interest are the ones at Fingest, Buckinghamshire, Earls Barton, Northamptonshire and Barnack, Cambridgeshire. All are far larger than would otherwise be necessary and it has been suggested that these were originally used as naves.

53 *Church, Fingest, Buckinghamshire*

The principal use of the tower was as a belfry but it is possible that many were built for defensive purposes. In East Anglia there are over 140 churches with round towers, many built in Saxon times and possibly intended for defence. Many originally had no direct link with the nave, which suggests that the church was not permanent. Moreover the only access to the tower was often 8–10 feet (2.4–3 metres) above the ground. At Bramfield in Suffolk the round tower is detached from the fourteenth-century nave and chancel. The walls of coursed flint and rubble are 5 feet (1.5 metres) thick, and run up to a later red-brick top course. It has lights which suggest a date of around 1175–1200; it is possible, however, that it was rebuilt then and that the base is eleventh-century.

54 *Saxon tower, Earls Barton, Northamptonshire*

55 *Church with round tower, Hales, Norfolk*

Clearly these towers could not have withstood a siege but they could provide temporary refuge for the villagers against marauding invaders. Other churches were certainly built with defence in mind: Shalfleet, Isle of Wight, which has walls 5 feet (1.5 metres) thick and had no external entrance until 1889; Great Salkeld, Cumbria, with its doorway at the west end of the nave barred and iron-clad; Newton Arlosh, also in Cumbria, with enormously thick walls, a narrow door opening and tiny slit windows; and at Bedale, North Yorkshire, where the staircase in the tower has grooves for a portcullis isolating the tower from the church.

Apart from the round towers, about eighty others in whole or in part are from the Saxon period. Many are of the campanile form, tall and narrow and undoubtedly derived from Italy. Many are roughly hewn with little or no decoration, for example Clapham, Bedfordshire. The most famous is the one at Earls Barton in Northamptonshire,

56 *Church tower, Shalfleet, Isle of Wight*

57 *Church, Newton Arlosh, Cumbria*

which has an elaborate decoration of pilaster strips and balusters to the openings. The capping of these towers would have been pyramidal but at Sompting in West Sussex there is a Saxon example of what is known as Rhenish helm.

Saxon characteristics are easily recognized in churches: walls are thin, often with long-and-short work to the quoins, windows are narrow with round or triangular heads, larger windows (especially belfry windows) are generally made up of two round-headed openings divided by a baluster-shaped mullion, doorways are tall and narrow with square jambs and semicircular or triangular heads with large impost blocks (later much reduced and sometimes roughly moulded), and walls sometimes have narrow projecting vertical strips of dressed stone (called pilaster strips) where freestone was commonly available.

The arrival of the Normans had little immediate impact on the building of the village churches. For half a century they concentrated on abbeys and cathedrals before turning their energies to the building, or rebuilding, of churches; the majority date from the second half of the twelfth century.

After the Conquest the Normans were apparently content to accept and adopt the nave-and-chancel plan. The simplest form involved a single cell with no structural division between nave and chancel, as at Little Braxted and Little Tey in Essex, North Marden in West Sussex and Winterborne Tomson in Dorset. Usually small Norman churches were of two cells, consisting of a nave and a narrower chancel, and the number still to be found testifies to the quality of their construction. They imported a new building style, which became Anglicized during the twelfth century, the Saxon tradition continuing alongside it with sometimes a Norman feature being included in what was otherwise a Saxon church. This can be seen to great effect on the tower at Bishopstone, East Sussex, which was built in around 1100; it is Saxon in appearance but with some Norman details. Similarly the round towers to be found in East Anglia are sometimes difficult to identify as either Saxon or Norman. Simple buildings like Heath Chapel, Shropshire, Stoke Orchard, Gloucestershire, and Prestbury, Cheshire (although this was largely rebuilt in 1747), and the later and more ornate ones like those at Adel, West Yorkshire, and Barfreston, Kent, remained nave-and-chancel churches but the Normans gave some village churches other plans and shapes. A slightly larger type had another cell between the nave and chancel, known as the choir, with each of the three compartments defined by arches. In this plan the chancel

58 *Norman chapel, Prestbury, Cheshire*

(or sanctuary) could be either square, as at Elkstone in Gloucestershire, or apsidal as at Kilpeck in Herefordshire, Wissington in Suffolk and Birkin in North Yorkshire. Sometimes a tower was used above the choir space, as at Stewkley in Buckinghamshire and Iffley in Oxfordshire. In addition they gave us aisleless cruciform churches with central towers and transepts, as at Stow in Lincolnshire, and churches with aisled naves and unaisled chancels, as at Castle Hedingham, Essex and Walsoken, Norfolk.

Over time the Normans transformed church building in England. The austere, high, narrow and dimly lit Saxon buildings, with their relatively slender walls, were gradually replaced with churches with thicker walls, rarely less than 2 feet 6 inches (75 cm), with an inner and outer skin of fairly well-laid rubble and a core consisting of a conglomeration of stones and mortar. The buildings themselves were of better proportions and with squatter, more substantial towers. They brought light with larger windows filled with glass, more complex columns, piers and arches, door openings deeply recessed, richly decorated on several orders of arches, with elaborate carving on the tympanum, and the first stone vaulting. The changes did not happen overnight; at first they imposed a uniform heavy style with dark, forbidding interiors. Piers were short, with square capitals and bases mounted with a semicircular arch, with little attempt at decoration, and it was only later that the style softened and the simple, rugged buildings gradually changed into a lighter style.

As long as the round arch remained there was little scope for further advancement in church architecture. It was not until the second half of the twelfth century that the first of the Gothic styles began to appear. From this time onwards Norman and Early English styles tended to become integrated until about 1300, when the Early English became almost universally adopted.

This style, though austere, has a simplicity that is intensely satisfying, its beauty never superseded. It has been described as something more than a style, more an art. It is distinguished by narrow, pointed windows called lancets, often formed into groups of two, three, five and even very occasionally seven. They were often stepped, the centre ones being higher than those flanking them, and all contained within a single arch. Tracery was not used at this time so any decoration was restricted to deeply cut mouldings. After the massive walls of the Norman period the Early English ones were thinner, pierced by more windows, thus providing more light in a taller more spacious building. Piers were usually circular, although octagonal and shafted ones are to be found, and bases often have water-hollow (deeply cut concave) mouldings – a most reliable clue to the period. Capitals were bell-shaped and deeply carved with foliage, stiff in the stalk much curved and lobed in the leaf.

Towers remained somewhat uncommon, and those that were built were usually square. Spires began to appear, growing, it seems, out of the original pyramidal cap. The earliest spires were developed in timber and by far the most common type is one in which the pyramidal cap is cut away from the base until eight sides are formed. Early examples are somewhat squat, but later they became taller and thinner. In many cases existing Saxon and Norman towers were raised and stone spires added. The earliest is at Barnack, Cambridgeshire, which was built around 1200 to cap the early eleventh-century tower. Four pinnacles were built at the corners abutting an octagonal drum surmounted by a modest spire. Later soaring broach spires like those at Polebrook, Northamptonshire, Gaddesby, Leicestershire, Ketton, Rutland, and Warboys, Cambridgeshire, began to appear.

59 *Church, Barnack, Cambridgeshire*

60 *Broach spire, Gaddesby, Leicestershire*

61 *Thirteenth-century church, Ketton, Rutland*

Although new churches were built – for instance Uffington, Oxfordshire, a rare twelfth-century Early English cruciform church, the later church at West Walton, Norfolk, built between 1225 and 1250, and those at Eaton Bray, Bedfordshire built around 1234–40 and Felmersham, also in Bedfordshire – much Early English work is to be found in adaptations or extensions of earlier churches. This can be seen at such churches as Stoke sub Hamdon, Somerset, where the Norman nave and chancel are tucked within Transitional and Early English transepts, with what can only be described as a bewildering array of windows, doors and corbels.

The Decorated style gradually grew out of the Early English style; the most obvious difference is in the tracery of the windows – first came the simple plate tracery, followed by geometrical, then reticulated, then finally a rich flowing tracery known as curvilinear. The churches themselves became less severe, with greater emphasis being placed on width rather than height. There was greater individuality, with the craftsmen and masons being able to express themselves in a way that they had been unable to do before. The country was becoming more prosperous, and ambitious churches such as Patrington, East Riding of Yorkshire, which was built between 1280 and 1360, and Heckington, Lincolnshire, an aisled cruciform church of the early fourteenth century, began to appear. Towers became more common and more elaborate, with such provisions as parapets, usually with a pinnacle at each corner. The combination of elegant towers and magnificent spires is a delightful focal point for many of our villages in stone-bearing areas of England. Now the broach spire was generally abandoned in favour of the more slender and graceful parapet spire as at Whittlesey, Cambridgeshire, and Stanton, Gloucestershire.

The Decorated style lasted for some seventy-five years starting in the reign of Edward I and coming to an abrupt end following the outbreak of the bubonic plague, known in this manifestation as the Black Death, which raged throughout 1348–9 and was responsible for the death of one-third of the population and the disappearance of some 3,000 villages. It virtually put a stop to all church building for a time and we will find few churches ascribed to the period 1350–1400.

When recovery came a great change passed over the spirit of English architecture, due in no small part to the altered conditions of life that followed in the wake of the Black Death, for the manorial

62 *Church, Stanton, Gloucestershire*

system broke down and there was insufficient labour for essential production, let along non-essential church-building. Up until this time the Gothic styles in England had followed a parallel course to those in France but now they diverged. In France, the Decorated style continued to become more elaborate, developing into the Flamboyant style but in England the Perpendicular evolved as a purely English style. As the name implies there is an emphasis on the vertical line and in particular the windows, with the mullions carried up to their heads. Windows became more obtuse, later often four-centred or even straight-headed.

In the fifteenth century the wealth of the nation increased and in those wealthier parts of England – the so-called wool areas of Lincolnshire, East Anglia, the East Riding of Yorkshire, Somerset and Gloucestershire – many churches were enlarged and magnificent new ones were built. It was a supreme building period for towers. Throughout the country they were built or rebuilt, larger, grander and more magnificent than ever before, although often less ornate than those of previous periods; they relied for their effect on proportion and outline. Such was the splendour of these towers that it was soon realized that spires were not required to complete them.

Although many new churches were built throughout the centuries, the village churches that we see today developed principally through the alteration and expansion of their original medieval plan; at first this may have been in response to the growth of the population and later in connection with the increase in church ritual. The nave-and-chancel plan continued to be used for many small village churches but throughout the country the aisled nave and the unaisled chancel established itself as the standard church plan throughout the Middle Ages. Although many churches were built to this plan it would, in many cases, be exceptional for them to reach such a relatively sophisticated point of development in a single initial building campaign. Saxon and Norman chancels were always small and many have been extended. Naves, too, were often extended westwards but from the thirteenth century onwards the provision of aisles became the commonest method of increasing the size of the church. With the introduction of aisles the nave was often raised above the arcade and pierced with a row of windows to provide light to the body of the church. Most of these clerestories date from the Perpendicular period. Towers were often added to the west end of the church and porches, which were not regarded as essential until the fourteenth century, were also added. From the close of the thirteenth century until the Dissolution in the sixteenth century the important and wealthy had chantry chapels built as extensions to the main structures, in some cases significantly affecting their development. For the less well off, religious or trade guilds were formed and these also often established their own chapels. Many churches also have a rectangular room to the north side of the church – the vestry, in which the vestments and vessels are kept and in which the priest robes. All these alterations and additions would have accrued over the centuries.

The medieval English styles began to come to an end with the Reformation. The Renaissance style then came in, although the Gothic tradition did not die out until well into the Stuart times. The church at Staunton Harold, Leicestershire, erected by Sir Robert Shirley in 1653–65 is decidedly Gothic, as is the one at Low Ham, Somerset, begun in 1620 but not finished until 1669 and the only remaining building in a deserted village. The Renaissance style was in this country an imitation of a style practised in Italy and western Europe and known in this country as Tudor, Elizabethan, Jacobean, Caroline and Stuart, according to the reigning sovereign. It lasted until the end of the seventeenth century.

Following the Dissolution of the Monasteries and the end of the Reformation little church-building was undertaken. Some churches were erected and added to during the latter years of Henry VIII's reign but they are few and far between and in the following reigns church-building virtually ceased. Elizabethan houses are quite common but complete Elizabethan churches rare; the brick church at Woodham Walter in Essex, built in 1563–4, is one example and the complete little church at Hulcote in Bedfordshire, built around 1590, is another. The first half of the seventeenth century saw little improvement, but some pleasant churches date from this period. The perfect little church at Sherrington, Wiltshire, was built in 1624 and incorporated some of the features of its medieval predecessors but its woodwork – benches, pulpit, communion rail and font – were made anew for a church which was finally decorated with painted cartouches surrounding texts. In the same year the delightful little brick church at Hoveton St Peter, Norfolk, was built. A larger and more ambitious church was built at Groombridge on the Kent-East Sussex border in 1623.

In the late seventeenth and early eighteenth century Classicism appeared following the Great Fire of London in 1666. The pillared, porticoed and steepled churches were part of Wren's rebuilding of London and were more of an urban style than a rural one. Wren's influence can however be seen in a number of our village churches. At Farley in Wiltshire the church, completed in 1690, is very much like a Wren building with its simple, pleasing brickwork and west tower. It was built for its founder, Sir Stephen Fox, by Alexander Fort, who was joiner to the Office of Works and worked for Wren. The church at Willen, Buckinghamshire, built in 1679–80 by Robert Hooke, who had assisted Wren in London, is another in the Wren style, as is the one at Gayhurst, also in Buckinghamshire, begun in 1728 and described as one of the classic-style treasures of the country. The church at Ingestre,

63 *Seventeenth-century church, Willen, Buckinghamshire*

Staffordshire, built in 1676, is more ambitious and was probably designed by Wren himself for Walter Chetwynd close to his house, Ingestre Hall. It is without doubt one of the most distinguished country churches of the Stuart period in England.

Classicism found its full expression in domestic architecture and many landowners required a church to match their grand new mansion. These were built so close by that they often appeared more like private chapels than parish churches. The small flint and stone church at Glynde, East Sussex, built in 1753–5 close to Glynde Place, which was owned and altered by Bishop Trevor in the 1750s and 1760s, is typical, as is the church at Great Witley, Worcestershire, consecrated in 1735. With the shell of Witley Court, which was burnt out in 1937, the latter forms an unforgettable pair.

Some landowners were more ambitious and designed churches to look like temples to be viewed from the great house as an 'eyecatcher'. One of the most ambitious is at Nuneham Courtenay in Oxfordshire, designed by the Earl of Harcourt and completed in 1764. Roman in style it is a domed temple with a pedimented portico supported on six Ionic columns and is lit by semicircular mullioned linnettes in the Palladian style. Others include those at Ayot St Lawrence, Hertfordshire, built in 1778–9, and Gunton, Norfolk, built to the design of Robert Adam in 1769. Georgian Gothick churches (not to be confused with the later Gothic revival churches) also became desirable landscape features. The church at Croome d'Abitot in Worcestershire was built in 1763, possibly by Lancelot Brown and Robert Adam, for the Earl of Coventry, and was obviously built to be viewed from the house, for it was placed on top of a hill – which was inconvenient for both house and village. Other patrons built churches in this style but without making them part of the land-scaped park. James Frampton built a notable church at Moreton, Dorset, in 1776, of which the tower is its finest feature, and when the Earl of Dorchester razed the small market town of Milton Abbas to the ground in 1786 and rebuilt a model village to replace it he built its own little church in Gothick style. It now forms part of the Picturesque village.

Gothick churches remained the exception and most village churches built in the late Georgian period (1760–1840) show a rich variety of classical designs while still retaining a good proportion of their original fittings. These little rural churches are always worth seeking out: Hardenhuish in Wiltshire is typical, built by the famous architect John Wood of Bath in 1779 of Bath stone, with a small steeple

64 *Eighteenth-century church, Glynde, East Sussex*

65 *Roman-style church, Nuneham Courtenay, Oxfordshire*

capped by a dome and some Venetian windows of clear glass. Others include Avington, Hampshire, Wolverton, Hampshire, Chislehampton, Oxfordshire. There are others which are more ambitious, for instance Brandsby, North Yorkshire, which has a cupola in the centre of the roof supported from beneath on Doric columns and at Kirkleatham, also in North Yorkshire, which was possibly designed by John Carr.

In the nineteenth century the Gothic revival took over from Classicism and church-building fell into the hands of professional architects who were unduly influenced by the Cambridge Camden Society. They insisted that the only place to worship was a Gothic building, preferably in the Middle Pointed style. With the expanding population, particularly in urban areas, there was a shortage of churches and in 1818 Parliament allocated £1,000,000 to build more, principally in urban areas. Further grants were made later and in no other time was there such a flood of church-building – not only new churches but the restoration and repair of existing ones. Most of the new churches were Gothic and most were built in the industrial towns. There were a few villages, however, where a patron might pay for a wholly new church like the one at Hoar Cross in Staffordshire, which was designed for Emily Meynell Ingram in memory of her husband by George Frederick Bodley and built between 1872–6, and the one at Eccleston in Cheshire which was built for the Duke of Westminster in 1899.

Nevertheless there is no denying the influence the great Victorian architects, such as Sir George Gilbert Scott (1811–78), George Frederick Bodley (1827–1907), George Edmund Street (1825–1881) and William Butterfield (1814–1900), had on many of our village churches with their restoration work. Although they are frequently criticized for the often unsympathetic alterations it must not be forgotten that prior to 1840 a great many churches were little more than dilapidated wrecks and that drastic measures were, indeed, necessary.

Churchyards

The church is usually situated within a churchyard, although a few, such as Fairfield in Kent, do not have one. Churchyards are often entered by means of a lych-gate, which marks the division between consecrated and unconsecrated ground. Its purpose was to enable the coffin to be set down on a stone or wooden table while part of the burial service was read and to provide shelter for bearers and mourners. Regrettably few coffin stones have survived; those at Bolney, West Sussex, Chiddingfold, Surrey, and Atherington and Ashprington in Devon are notable exceptions. The word 'lych' derives from the Anglo-Saxon for corpse. In medieval times few churchyards would be without a lych-gate of some kind; some had two and at Troutbeck, Cumbria, there are three. Few lych-gates older than the seventeenth century now exist; those at Limpsfield, Surrey, Boughton Monchelsea, Kent, Whitbourne, Worcestershire, Woolhope, Herefordshire and Isleham, Cambridgeshire, all date from the fifteenth and sixteenth centuries, but these are rare and all have been extensively repaired.

66 *Church at Fairfield, Kent*

67 *Lych-gate, Woolhope, Herefordshire*

Although some lych-gates were made of stone, such as the one at St Just-in-Roseland in Cornwall, the majority were of timber or with stone bases and timber superstructures, and many would have decayed over the centuries. In the eighteenth century, when their use declined, they were demolished rather than repaired, often being replaced by timber or iron gates. Sometimes central pivots or tapsels were provided, allowing the pall bearers to pass either side with the coffin in the middle. At Duntisbourne Abbots, Gloucestershire, and at Down St Mary, Devon, provision was made for the coffin to rest on top of the gate. Most lych-gates to be found today are not of great age; many were rebuilt in the nineteenth century but they still add such charm to many village churchyards.

Not all lych-gates are independent structures; access to the churchyard may be through a passage within or under a building. Usually these buildings are cottages, with the upper floor of one being carried over, as at Penshurst in Kent. At Finchingfield in Essex the building is the former guildhall. In some instances the lych-gate is an independent structure with a room or rooms above which might have been used by a priest, as a schoolroom, as a parish room or as a library. The one at Long Compton in Warwickshire is a fine example.

68 *Lych-gate, St Just-in-Roseland, Cornwall*

69 *Lych-gate, Long Compton, Warwickshire*

Before the Reformation every churchyard would have been dominated by a freestanding cross. They were erected to signify the sanctity of the consecrated ground and they were important for, in the days before gravestones, they were the only memorial to all the departed. They were also used as a station on the processional path, and proclamations were made and business transactions conducted there. Remains are fairly common, particularly in those areas where good stone is abundant, but many were destroyed by Cromwell's men during the Civil War, who felt that such works were idolatrous and broke off and removed the heads which bore sculptured images, leaving only the steps and part of the shaft. However, some still survive, for instance those at Somerby in Lincolnshire, the fourteenth-century one at Ashleworth in Gloucestershire, and the one at Bishops Lydeard in Somerset. Some have been restored: the gabled head at Ampney Crucis in Gloucestershire, was removed and walled up inside the entrance to the rood loft, where it was discovered during restoration work and restored to the cross in around 1860. Similarly, at Tyberton, Herefordshire, the gable head was removed and hidden in the roof of the old church and the shaft buried, and it was only comparatively recently that the gable head was discovered and restored to its shaft.

70 *Churchyard cross, Tyberton, Herefordshire*

The oldest crosses were carved monoliths, and these are to be found mainly in Cornwall and the North. There are some 300 of these crosses, some of great antiquity, reaching as far back as the Celtic missionaries. They are often difficult to date for, although they are often elaborately carved, there is usually no inscription.

Headstones from before the seventeenth century are very rare for the majority of the population were interned in only a shroud tied at the head and foot, with no marker on the grave except a wooden cross, which would soon decay and disappear. It was not until the seventeenth century, as wealth increased, that there was a desire among those who could afford it to buy plots and have their resting place on earth noted in some way. Local materials were used: stone and slates, where they were available, but elsewhere timber and, where iron-smelting occurred, such as the Weald of Sussex and Kent and later in the Coalbrookdale area of Shropshire, iron. It was not until the nineteenth century, with the introduction of white marble from Italy followed by polished black marble and multicoloured chips, that the visual harmony of many of our village churchyards was spoilt.

The finest headstones are Georgian. This was the great age of the English tombstone, a period of good design and better-executed inscriptions. Those in the Cotswolds are specially notable, and some of the finest chest tombs, including such Cotswold innovations as the bale tomb, in which a large semi-cylindrical stone covers most of the ledger, and the so-called tea-caddy tomb, are to be found there. Painswick, Gloucestershire, is regarded as the finest churchyard in England but many other Cotswold churchyards contain examples of these finely carved monuments. Not all areas were so fortunate, and where no stone was available timber was used, particularly in parts of the Home Counties. By the seventeenth century timber gravelboards, sometimes referred to as 'bedheads', were introduced, consisting of two posts supporting the ends of a board on which the deceased's name and a text was placed. This type of memorial persisted well into the nineteenth century and is still to be found, although they are becoming rarer each year.

Mausoleums are found in a few churchyards. They are often imposing architectural structures dominating the churchyard and housing the bodies of important families when there was no longer room to house them within the church.

There are other structures to be found within the churchyard. Watchboxes were at one time built there to house armed men during the night to guard against body-snatchers who would, under the cover of darkness, exhume the bodies of newly buried people for anatomical studies. A few still remain, for instance at Doddington, Northumberland, while Warblington, Hampshire, has two small brick and flint boxes, one at each side of the churchyard.

At one time it was common to go to church on horseback and on occasions stables were provided to feed and shelter the horses during the long services. At Brailsford, Derbyshire, there is a brick one dated 1754; another stands close by the lych-gate at East Peckham in Kent, which still contains the stalls and the names of the gentry who used them painted above. At Wingfield, Suffolk, is another stable, this time with a mounting platform. Mounting blocks are also to be found at the entrances to many churchyards.

Pillar sundials are also a feature; in some cases they have been

71 *Bell cage, Wrabness, Essex*

mounted on the broken shaft of a medieval cross, others have been purpose made. The most remarkable is the seventeenth-century one at Elmley Castle, Worcestershire. Not all churches had belfries to house their bells and in a few cases bell cages were provided for them. The most famous is the timber-framed one at East Bergholt, Suffolk, which holds five bells. A much smaller structure stands in the churchyard at Wrabness, Essex, and contains only one. Graveside doles were at one time fairly common, and often the tops of chest tombs situated close to the south porch were used for the distribution of bread, but in a few instances dole tables were constructed to distribute the charity. The one at Powerstock, Dorset, is said to date from the thirteenth century.

Nonconformist Chapels

After the Reformation and Henry VIII's break with the Pope the newly established Church of England did not satisfy everyone. The dissenters can be divided into two groups: the Puritans, who wished to reform the established Church from within, and the Separatists, who saw no alternative but to leave it and set up new independent units. Some 2,000 clergy, lecturers and fellows, unable to accept the conditions laid down in the Act of Uniformity of 1662, were ejected from their livings in England and Wales. In the years between the Restoration of the Monarchy in 1660 and the Toleration Act of 1689 the penalties for attending such meetings were harsh. At first the chapels built by these Nonconformists were often modest, unassuming buildings, situated either away from the village or on its edge; it was not until late in the eighteenth century, when Nonconformity had grown and both its legal and social position was secure, that the chapel became a prominent feature in many villages.

Three main groups of dissenters developed; first the independents (later to become the Congregationalists), followed by the Baptists, who were first identified in 1603, and then the Presbyterians, who were at first moderate Puritans within the Church of England before leaving and forming their own chapels. After the Toleration Act of 1689 came the Unitarians, followed by the Methodists from 1739. Within these main groups there were many divisions. The Congregational Union was formed in 1832 but individual churches still retained their individual autonomy; in the seventeenth century the Baptists had two main groups, the General Baptists who believed in free will, and the Particular Baptists who believed in predestination: the Methodists, who at first had not considered themselves as dissenters, later formed their own church before dividing into a number of separate churches on the death of John Wesley in 1791. It was not until 1932 that the largest of these – the United, the Primitive and the Wesleyan – joined to form the Methodist Church. In 1974 the Congregationalists and the Presbyterians united to form the United Reformed Church.

Apart from these major Nonconformist chapels, there were many smaller denominations. Some were national, such as the Plymouth Brethren, the Countess of Huntingdon's and the Bible Christians, and others were local, such as the Peculiar People of Essex, some of whose small and simple chapels still remain, and the Cokelers or Society of Dependants of Sussex.

At first these Nonconformist groups met in private houses of the faithful, or in barns, or even in the open air, and there are still chapels that retain the domestic style of their origins. One example is in the Norfolk village of Gressenhall. It originated as a barn and the attached house was probably a farmhouse. It was first used as a place of worship in the early part of the nineteenth century by the Methodists, and was purchased by the United Methodist Church in 1923 before being brought into the Methodist Church in 1932. It is still known locally as 'God's Cottage'.

Some chapels are actual converted houses, such as the Congregational chapel at Walpole, Suffolk, which was originally built in 1607 as a house before being converted into a chapel in 1647 and enlarged some time before 1698. Others are often attached to other buildings, for instance the Methodist chapel at Willersey, Gloucestershire, which forms part of a perfect row of Cotswold stone cottages. The Baptist chapel at Loughwood, a remote spot near Dalwood, Devon, would from the outside be taken for a schoolhouse. Records extend back to 1653, when it was built for the Baptist congregation of Kilmington and the present structure certainly dates back to this time. The Spartan interior is mainly of early eighteenth-century date, with white walls and a barrel vault ceiling, scrubbed pine floorboards and pews, and is wonderfully preserved. A tall pulpit dominates one end and beneath it is the baptismal tank, hidden by floorboards. Behind the pulpit are two retiring rooms, one for each sex and each with a tiny fireplace. A small stable is sited alongside. The building is now owned by the National Trust.

72 *Congregational chapel, Walpole, Suffolk*

73 *Baptist chapel, Loughwood, Devon*

Chapels built before 1689 are rare, for prior to this date Puritans were liable to legal penalties for holding unauthorized religious meetings. The oldest one, said to have been built in 1566, is at Horningsham, Wiltshire, and was built with the permission of Sir John Thynne so that the Scottish masons he employed in the construction of Longleat could hold their own services in accordance with their Presbyterian tradition. Later it became Congregationalist, and so it remains today. It was altered in about 1700 and again in the nineteenth century but still retains the domestic appearance of those early country chapels. One of the earliest Baptist chapels is at Cote, Oxfordshire, and dates from 1664.

A feature of Presbyterian chapels is that they have bell-cots at the west end. An early example is to be found at Bramhope in West Yorkshire. It was built in 1649, at a time when the Presbyterians were still within the Church of England, and the plain, rectangular building of rubble stone with its belfry at one end is typical. It was badly damaged in 1962 and has since been carefully restored. The interior still has the three-decker pulpit with reading desk below and sounding board above.

After the Toleration Act, chapel-building could commence, with the domestic style slowly being replaced by a more formal, but still simple kind of architecture, which externally had no ecclesiastical features. Congregational, Baptist, Unitarian and occasionally Presbyterian chapels were built throughout England, but in many rural areas dissent was never very widespread; indeed the eighteenth century saw a general weakening of dissent in England. In rural areas chapels continued to be converted from barns or cottages; the Baptist chapel at Great Warford, Cheshire, is typical, having been converted from a barn and a cottage in about 1712. This practice continued for over a hundred years as with the Baptist chapel at Keysoe Row, Bedfordshire, which was converted from a small late-eighteenth century barn in 1808.

There were two periods of intense chapel-building at either end of the eighteenth century: first with the evangelical revival and then with the spread of Methodism. It lasted throughout the nineteenth century and into the early part of the twentieth, when chapels became generally more formal in their appearance. The materials varied from corrugated iron, weatherboarding, local brick or stone. The architecture remained simple and can be dismissed as commonplace, but at their best they have an ecclesiastical symmetry that can be most enjoyable. Most were unpretentious rectangular structures with a single door and plain windows. They were often of red brick regardless of the village's local materials and styles and sometimes sat a little unhappily in the landscape. The chapel at Newbiggin, County Durham, is typical of this simple design; after initially meeting in local farmhouses the Methodists built a chapel in 1760 and it is said to be the oldest Methodist chapel in continuous use. John Wesley often preached there. Its present character, and that of the adjacent school, owe much to the rebuilding of 1860 when the front was raised. The Congregational chapel at Ravenstonedale, Cumbria, is another typical example. Built in 1726 and altered in 1868, when the windows were enlarged, it remains a simple structure.

A few were a little more ambitious, including the fine mid-eighteenth century Unitarian chapel at Stannington, a village near the edge of the moorland to the west of Sheffield, with a chapel-keeper's cottage attached at one end, the octagonal Methodist chapel at Heptonstall,

74 *Congregational chapel, Ravenstonedale, Cumbria*

West Yorkshire, which was built in 1764, the one at Fressingfield, Suffolk, a Strict Baptist chapel built in 1835 and shaped like a coffin, and the Lana Wesleyan chapel at Pancrasweek in Devon, built in 1838 and the most attractive of Devon's chapels. Towards the end of the nineteenth century Nonconformity began to gain respectability and many chapels, particularly in towns, were built to look like Anglican churches, often with a Gothic appearance.

As we have seen, chapels are rather plain sombre buildings, so the Congregational chapel at Roxton, Bedfordshire, with its mock-rustic *cottage orné* style comes as a surprise. Originally a barn it was converted by Charles Metcalfe, the local squire, and given the appearance of a *cottage orné* with a deep thatched roof, a tree-trunk colonnade, white rendered walls and ogee-pointed windows and doors. Opened in 1808, it was visible from Metcalfe's house and was meant as an ornament to his estate as well as a place with a serious use. Two wings were added later in the same style, one containing the Sunday school, the other the village school.

75 *Unitarian chapel, Stannington, South Yorkshire*

The basic requirements of a Nonconformist chapel were simple, for all that was required was a large, open barn-like structure with windows to the two side walls and a front wall with an entrance door, often protected by a vestibule and perhaps with windows on either side. Facing the entrance was often a blank wall, in the middle of which stood the pulpit, a characteristic feature of almost every kind of Nonconformist chapel, from which the minister would conduct the entire proceedings unless it was a communion service. Sometimes on either side of the pulpit were windows. In front of the pulpit was the plain communion table on a dais, at which the minister and deacons or elders sat when distributing the elements to the congregation. The body of the chapel was taken up with rows of pews, which were often not much more than benches although, on occasions, they might have had some style or might even have been box pews. There was probably an organ or harmonium on one side but no statues and sacred paintings

76 *Lana Wesleyan chapel,
Pancrasweek, Devon*

77 *Congregational chapel, Roxton, Bedfordshire*

were to be found, such was the Protestants' distrust of iconography. The only example of religious art might be an illuminated text painted on the wall above the pulpit. Contrast this simple interior with that of the parish church with its nave, pillars, clerestory, screens, chancels and stained glass.

Today, like many other village buildings, many of these Nonconformist chapels have become redundant. A small but significant number are in the care of charitable trusts, but many others have been demolished or remain empty or have been found other uses. Some have been adapted for use as village halls, youth clubs, warehouses and even occasionally workshops or factories, while others have been converted into houses. In all these cases, with the inevitable loss of fittings much of their historical value has been destroyed.

Friends' Meeting Houses

A distinct group of buildings is the meeting houses for Quakers. They can hardly be classified as chapels and in fact Quakers never called them anything other than meeting houses, for all that was required was a room in which to meet and benches to sit on. Many smaller meeting houses reflect this simple need.

It was in the early 1650s that George Fox founded the Religious Society of Friends and like other Nonconformists they at first suffered severe persecution. Like other dissenters, therefore, they initially held their meetings in private houses or barns. It was not until later that purpose-built meeting houses began to appear and these were generally of a domestic style. Research by David Butler in 1985 shows that 90 percent of all meeting houses built in the first hundred years of the Society, 60 percent of those built in its second century and 35 percent of those built in its third century were of a vernacular or cottage style.

The earliest meeting houses are all of this type; the one at Almeley Wooton, Herefordshire, dates from around 1672 and is a black-and-white timber-framed building characteristic of the area. Others include the ones at Briggflatts, near Sedbergh, Cumbria (1675), West Adderbury, Oxfordshire (1675), Jordans, near Chalfont St Giles, Buckinghamshire (1688), Fairfield, near Skipton, North Yorkshire

(1689), and Come-to-Good (the name is a corruption of the Cornish Cwm-ty-Coit meaning the combe by the dwelling in the wood), Kea, Cornwall (1708). These are all purpose-built but many of the early ones were either conversions or extensions to existing houses, like Blue Idol, Thakeham, West Sussex, which was a timber-framed building built around 1600 with a meeting room added at one end in 1691.

Many early Quaker meeting houses had two doors in a symmetrical long wall, with a pulpit in the centre of the wall opposite, and a gallery or loft on two or three sides. The two doors were essential, as the seating formed a central block in front of the pulpit with no central aisle. By the latter part of the eighteenth century the domestic type of building changed and standard forms of meeting houses were constructed following the example of other denominations' chapels. However these are generally to be found in towns.

78 *Meeting house, Briggflatts, Cumbria*

79 *Meeting house, Come-to-Good, Kea, Cornwall*

There were some requirements peculiar to the Quakers. A normal feature in all but the latest meeting houses, is the ministers' stand, a raised platform of up to three tiers on one side of the room, in which the ministers (a role abolished in the 1920s), elders and overseers sat facing the other members. It could be placed in the centre or along the full width of the wall. They are now no longer used, for everyone, irrespective of their function, sits around a table in the centre of the room. In most cases a separate room was provided for women, often divided from the men by a partition which could be removed to form one room when required. A loft was another feature, particularly in the south-west of England, which was often the women's room. Several country meeting houses also had stables, for instance Brant Broughton, Lincolnshire, which dates from 1701, and at Briggflatts there is a pen for members' dogs.

80 *Meeting house, Blue Idol, Thakeham, West Sussex*

FOUR

Village Houses

The nature of village houses has changed greatly over the centuries, for they reflect the ever-changing way of life of the people who occupy them. In medieval times only the village church and the manor house would have been built to survive the centuries, for the majority of houses would have been of frail construction, using materials found close at hand, probably only of one room and affording little comfort for their inhabitants. The majority of our existing village houses date from the end of the sixteenth century onwards, when the older, flimsily constructed dwellings were swept away in what W.G. Hoskins has termed the 'rebuilding of rural England', to be replaced with more substantial ones. Over much of the country the period of this rebuilding ran from 1570 to 1640, but further north, in Cumbria, Northumberland and County Durham, it occurred somewhat later.

In many villages today the church will be medieval, the manor house will date from the Middle Ages to the sixteenth century, substantial farmhouses will date from the sixteenth to the seventeenth centuries, the houses of merchants and professional people will be eighteenth-century, and those of labourers, artisans and the like, nineteenth century. This is of course an over-simplification; in many cases, particularly in the South-west and in Essex, Suffolk and the adjoining parts of Hertfordshire and Cambridgeshire, many of the older houses – manor houses and medieval farmhouses – were abandoned for new dwellings away from the village, while the older houses were divided into tenements. William Harrison, Rector of Radwinter in Essex in the reign of Queen Elizabeth I, wrote of the dwellings in his time:

> In old time the houses of the Britons were slightly set-up with few posts and many rattles with stable and all offices under one roof, the like whereof almost is to be seen in fenny countries and northern parts unto this day, where for the lack of wood they are enforced to continue this ancient manner of building.

This general rebuilding was brought to a sudden end with the outbreak of the Civil War in 1642 and it was not until the 1660s, following the Restoration, that the momentum was regained.

In the South-east and eastern England from the end of the sixteenth century onwards, the old timber-framed houses of the previous centuries began to be modernized to afford the inhabitants greater comfort. Many were clad with plaster, tiles, weatherboarding and brick to provide a house that was warmer and less draughty and damp. New fashionable sash windows and panelled doors often completed the modernization. In addition many old houses of one and a half storeys were raised to provide additional accommodation. New houses throughout the country, whether of stone, timber or brick, were constructed incorporating these refinements from the start, while new plans developed to provide more comfortable and compact houses. House types popular during the sixteenth and seventeenth centuries, began to be displaced by designs that were more symmetrical. By the beginning of the eighteenth century houses of five bays, with a symmetrical façade, began to appear in our villages and, with the continuing enclosures of the open fields, elsewhere in the countryside. The development and improvement of the village house was a gradual process, for many of the old concepts, developed over the centuries, were often retained, but the two main factors in their evolution were the desires for more comfort and greater privacy. To these can be added the desire to proclaim the family's status, requiring them to live in a house which reflected their wealth and position. The history of the English house is one of continuing change.

Medieval Houses

The universal feature of the medieval manor house was the open hall, and this remained so up until the sixteenth century. It was always the largest, and sometimes the only room in the house, open from the ground floor to the apex of the roof, and in early times, the owner, his family, his guests and his servants or retainers all ate, slept and entertained here. It was also where the manorial court was held, where local disputes relating to the manor were tried and settled. The court probably sat several times a year and at these sessions the lord of the manor would receive any fines due to him. Near the centre of this room was the open hearth on which fires were lit, the smoke escaping, as best it could through small gablets at the junction of the hips and gables, or else through a louvre in the roof. Beyond the hearth was the 'upper end' occupied by the family, which contained the high table and bench for meals. At the other end, the 'lower end', lived the servants and retainers. The social division between family and servants was marked by the central open truss.

The earliest of these open-hall houses were of aisled construction and were almost certainly of manorial status. Based on the available evidence, they consisted of only a two-bay aisled hall without any other rooms. This simplest form persisted to the end of the thirteenth century. A two-storey extension was added to the lower end, either built in series or else as a projecting cross-wing, containing a buttery and pantry on the ground floor and a chamber, probably the solar, on the floor above for the private use of the family. Between the hall and the service wing was the screens passage. Further up the social scale were houses with an extension or cross-wing at each end.

Aisled halls are to be found mainly in eastern and south-east England, but by the middle of the fourteenth century this construction had generally been abandoned, for the arcade post restricted the clear floor area and thus proved to be inconvenient. In eastern England uninterrupted floor space was achieved by other means: at Tiptofts Manor, Wimbish, Essex, which was built in the fourteenth century, an elementary form of hammer-beam was used to support the arcade plate. Another answer to the problem was a raised aisle, in which the truncated aisle posts were supported on a large tie-beam. In the south-east and in the west, particularly Herefordshire and Worcestershire, base crucks began to be used to support the central truss, thus removing the encumbrance of the arcade posts.

With the decline of the manorial system the importance of the open hall declined and by the fifteenth century aisled construction and its related forms had generally been abandoned for domestic purposes. The medieval plan, however, with its hall – now often quite small – still open to the roof and flanked at one or both ends by a two-storey bay, with a screens passage between the hall and the lower end, remained the standard type. Unlike houses of aisled construction these later hall houses of south-east and eastern England rarely have cross-wings projecting beyond the face of the hall, although generally the upper storeys of these end bays are jettied, usually to the front only. In eastern England these jettied upper storeys were given their own ridged roofs, set at right angles to the roof of the hall, and so in effect the eaves to the hall remained lower than the eaves of the cross-wing.

In south-east England, particularly in Kent around Maidstone, another type evolved, known as the Wealden house. The basic plan remained as elsewhere, although the screens passage was more clearly defined, often by a separate narrow bay. It is externally that the main difference occurred, for instead of the roof being in three separate parts with three separate ridges the complete house was covered under a single steeply pitched hipped roof with one ridge line. Jettied end chambers continued to be used but the front line of the eaves continued across the front of the hall to produce extra deep projecting eaves. Generally these projecting eaves were supported by curved brackets at each end and in the centre of the main tie-beam of the hall roof. The origin of these Wealden houses is obscure, but they appeared at some date from around 1400 reaching their peak about eighty years later and continuing to be built for about another fifty years. Although they are found in the Weald the highest concentration is to the east of Maidstone. Old Bell Farm, in the village of Harrietsham, Kent, is one of the finest examples; built in the late fifteenth century it still retains its original front entrance door and four-centred arch, three doors in the screens passage, a crown-post roof and one of its solid block stairs. Externally the central recess is coved, the bressummers to the jettied end chambers moulded and the two-storeyed bay window to the hall glazed.

81 *Wealden house, Hawkenbury Farm, Headcorn, Kent*

Although the majority of open-hall houses are in eastern and south-east England, there are houses of similar date and size to be found elsewhere in the country. Yelford Manor, near Bampton in Oxfordshire is one which has changed little over the centuries. It was built for the Hastings family, on a moated site next to the church, with an open hall which still occupies the centre of the building.

Before the sixteenth century the great majority of houses were built of timber, even in those areas that we now associate with the stone tradition, for instance the Cotswolds. Smaller open-hall houses of stone are therefore less common in rural areas and would have been built for men of some substance. One excellent example is Northborough Manor, Cambridgeshire, built possibly around 1340 for Robert de Northborough, Bishop of Lichfield and, for a short period, Treasurer

82 *Yelford Manor, Oxfordshire*

of England. The house is not particularly large but would have been a substantial building in its day. The hall is virtually intact, but the cross-wings have been rebuilt. In the seventeenth century the hall was ceiled over to provide an additional floor and a dormer window inserted. In the 1970s the inserted floor was removed returning the open hall to its original form. Another early open-hall house of note is to be found in the village of Nassington in Northamptonshire; the Prebendal Manor House was built as the residence of a Prebend of Lincolnshire Cathedral in the thirteenth century on the site of one of King Canute's royal manors.

Most medieval houses were designed for ground-floor living, but there were those which for some reason, usually defensive, had the living quarters on the first floor, the ground floor usually being used only for storage. Two types developed: the first-floor-hall house, which was Norman in origin, and the tower house.

83 *Northborough Manor, Cambrideshire*

Apart from the occasional town house most first-floor-hall houses are manorial or religious in origin. The basic plan was simple: on the first floor was the hall, usually of two bays, and at one end a single-bay solar, both open to the roof. Access to the hall was by means of an external staircase. The hall was heated by a fireplace located on either the rear or the side wall, but the solar was usually unheated. The ground floor was generally an open space, used for storage, with an external door and a small window for ventilation. Perhaps the most complete example is to be found at Boothby Pagnell in Lincolnshire, which was built around the end of the twelfth century. The layout is much as it was when it was first built, although the house would not originally have stood alone; there would have been a number of outbuildings, including a detached kitchen. Most known examples of these are constructed of stone, and were built between about 1150 and 1300, but there are some similar to them that were constructed of timber.

84 *First-floor-hall house, Boothby Pagnell, Lincolnshire*

The tower or pele house was also defensible. It differed from first-floor-hall houses in that, instead of the accommodation being confined to the first floor, there was a second and even occasionally a third floor. The ground floor, usually vaulted, was used solely for storage or perhaps as a service area. Access to this area was by means of a stout door capable of being barred from the inside in case of attack. Above this was the main living room or hall, with the solar above this, and, in a few cases, a further chamber above that. Unlike first-floor-hall houses there was no external stairway; access between the floors was by means of a stone staircase located in one corner or in a projecting turret, or, in a few cases, a straight flight within the thickness of the wall. Access to the roof was also possible, where the parapet walls were often corbelled and battlemented, leaving a walkway around the gable roof.

The earliest pele houses date from the fourteenth century and continued to be built until the late sixteenth century in the debatable country between England and Scotland. Many have been abandoned and have disappeared or become derelict, but a good number still survive, incorporated within later buildings. A fine example is to be found at Elsdon, Northumberland. It was probably built late in the fourteenth century, not for the Lords of the Manor, the de Umfraville family, but for the parson. Like other tower houses it has a stone

85 *Pele house, Elsdon, Northumberland*

86 *Pele house, Long Horsley, Northumberland*

vaulted ground floor and two floors above. Only in the eighteenth century did the inhabitants build a comfortable, modern house alongside the old one. Probably of sixteenth-century date is the one at Long Horsley, also in Northumberland.

Post-medieval Houses

The period from the middle of the sixteenth century to the outbreak of the Civil War was one of great economic growth. For the first time since the Black Death the population was rising again and demand was increasing from the expanding towns. With Henry VIII's break from

Rome and the subsequent dissolution of the general monasteries in 1539, vast tracts of land passed into the ownership of the King and was subsequently distributed by Henry and, later, Elizabeth to the nobility, gentry and other receivers of wealth. Many took advantage of their new-found wealth by abandoning their old manor houses within the villages to build grander ones some distance away. As trade and commerce grew, both nationally and abroad, large houses were also built by the newly rich merchants and financiers, who were keen to impress the established gentry. Tudor and Jacobean country houses, built of stone, brick and timber, are to be found throughout the country, and they stand at the overlap between the medieval house and the Classical buildings of later centuries.

The innovations made by the nobility, the gentry and the rising professional and merchant classes in their homes were soon taken up by local builders and, for the first time, small yeoman farmers and husbandmen were building their houses with more durable materials. As the price of agricultural produce rose, many small producers were able to increase their output by improved farming practices and by co-operating in the enclosure of the old open fields. Yeoman farmers began to accumulate money often buying out their neighbours and so building up substantial farms. Even tenant copyholders were finding their fixed rents less onerous as their income rose.

The dominant feature in the medieval house, from the largest manor house to the humblest cottage, was the open hall, which was the centre of life for the entire household. In the sixteenth century the desire for greater privacy and comfort led to the abandonment of the open hall and the introduction of the chimney stack. It could be argued that the development of the chimney was the greatest single advance in living conditions in the sixteenth century, enabling the family to enjoy a number of heated rooms instead of huddling around a central hearth.

Many old open halls had a new floor inserted and at the same time a chimney and fireplace was built. The space gained upstairs was often only large enough for storage, but sometimes dormers would be provided or the external walls raised and a new roof constructed to create full-height rooms. The former mullioned window to the hall was often replaced by a glazed bay window lighting both rooms. These are today a feature of many Wealden houses.

With the abandonment of the open hall, new house types began to appear, but it must be remembered that the open hall's influence lasted

long after it had disappeared and, although it was no longer open to
the roof, it retained many of its former attributes. From the early
sixteenth century houses of two full storeys began to be built in south-
east England, although sometimes this would only be a single storey
with an attic. Elsewhere, older forms, more closely related to open
halls, continued. One such was the longhouse in which both men and
animals were housed under a single roof, with the house and byre
separated by a cross-passage or cross-walk with a door at each end.
Longhouses were an ancient upland house type, and from excavations
in Devon and Cornwall appear to date from at least the eleventh or
twelfth century. Early examples had an open hall but later an upper
floor was provided throughout. Access to both house and byre
remained a feature; Shilstone, Throwleigh, which is dated 1656 and is
one of the last longhouses to be built in Devon, still retains access
to the byre from the cross-passage. Later many old longhouses were

87 *Shilstone, Throwleigh, Devon*

modified to incorporate a separate entrance into the house. Towards the end of the seventeenth century, at a time when longhouses on Dartmoor had ceased to be built and earlier ones were being altered and modernized, they were still the preferred design in other parts of the country. One such area was North Yorkshire and another was Cumbria, but it seems likely that other upland areas also had this form.

A variation of the longhouse was the linear form, with the house and farm buildings in two or more contiguous buildings, each with its own entrance but sharing the same roof line. They began to appear in the highland zone when the traditional longhouse was in decline; most appear to date from the late seventeenth century and can be found in many of the villages of Cumbria and North Yorkshire, in the southern part of the Pennines in Derbyshire, the adjoining parts of Staffordshire and Cheshire, as well as in the south-west and north-east of England.

The cross-passage was the predominant feature of all late medieval houses of more than one room, and it remained the most characteristic post-medieval feature throughout the seventeenth and eighteenth centuries. This was particularly true of south-west, western and north-west England, parts of the limestone belt (the Cotswolds and northern Somerset), the Pennines and many other areas. The commonest plan is of a house with three rooms in line, normally comprising a service area, an entry passage flanked by the fireplace of the principal room, a hall or, later, a hall-kitchen and a further room, the parlour, beyond. There were many variants to this basic plan, most relating to the position of the chimney: in the lowland zone it was placed away from the cross-passage between the hall and the parlour, so heating both rooms, while in the south-west it was often placed on the front wall of the hall where it served as a status symbol. Like many other older houses of all kinds, some were extended by raising the walls and roof to enlarge the attic to a full storey height. Cross-bays were sometimes added to form the classic lowland T or L plan.

As we have seen, the underlying feature of most houses up to the seventeenth century was the screens or cross-passage, with the living quarters to one side and the service rooms to the other. These so-called divided houses were replaced by superior types, in which the service rooms were incorporated within the house. The first, and by far the most popular, of these undivided houses was the baffle or lobby-entry plan, which gained popularity in the south-east before spreading into East Anglia and then into the south and the Midlands and finally, in the eighteenth century, into the remaining parts of the country. Of these the most common form, particularly in the lowland zone, was the central-lobby house in which the entrance was towards the centre of the front lateral wall and led into a small lobby between two main rooms, the hall and parlour, by the insertion of an axial chimney stack. The advantage of this simple plan over those houses with a cross-passage, was that it provided greater comfort by reducing draughts as well as providing independent access to both rooms. In addition, with the central stack, both living rooms could be heated.

88 *Central-lobby house, Barking, Suffolk*

89 *Farmhouse, Carlton Husthwaite, North Yorkshire*

From this basic plan the classic central-lobby-entrance house developed, which was almost universally adopted for all new larger houses in south-east and eastern England. These houses comprised three ground-floor rooms: a heated parlour, a heated main room (hall or hall-kitchen) and, at the opposite end to the parlour, an unheated service room, with the entrance lobby between the parlour and main room. The entrance to the service room was directly from the main room and it was commonly divided into two. The stack was usually placed centrally within the depth of the house, the return wall forming one wall of the entrance lobby – the one opposite the entrance door – with the stairs positioned between the stack and rear lateral wall. Such was the popularity of this house type that many older houses with cross-passages were converted, inserting an axial stack within the bay of the passage.

Double-pile Houses

∾

In all the houses previously described the common feature was that the main part was only one room deep, although some rooms may have been divided laterally, and the service rooms were in nearly all cases subdivided. At the beginning of the seventeenth century this medieval concept began to change, having lasted for over 500 years. The service rooms, perhaps the kitchen or buttery, were located at the rear, housed in a continuous outshut under a catslide roof. Generally these were adaptations of earlier houses, but towards the end of the seventeenth century an entirely new type evolved. It was a complete break with the past, with the house two-storeyed throughout and the service rooms to the rear. The gentry first began to build this type in the middle of the seventeenth century under the influence of Inigo Jones, Surveyor of Works to James I and Charles I. Externally these buildings were plain, often to the point of austerity, and their appeal relied on their symmetry, the pleasing proportion of their tall windows and the use of cornices and balustrades. They stand in striking contrast to the ornate houses of the Jacobean era.

By the first half of the eighteenth century these double-pile houses, with their symmetrical façades, had become the standard design for the prosperous farmers, the better off parsons and the increasing number of merchants and professional people. Unlike most earlier styles which were more popular in one region than another, the double-pile house gained popularity throughout the country at more or less the same time, owing no doubt, in part, to the increasing number of pattern books available to country builders.

Most double-pile houses had four ground floor rooms: two principal living rooms at the front and at the rear a kitchen and another service room. In almost all cases the living rooms were deeper than the service rooms. In southern areas the staircase was in the entrance lobby between the two living rooms, while in the north it was generally located at the rear, between the two service rooms. The front entrance was placed more or less centrally along the front elevation and opened either into an entrance lobby, with direct access to the dining room and parlour, or directly into one of the living rooms. A great advantage of this type was that, for the first time, both living rooms, as well as the service rooms, could be heated by fireplaces situated on the gable walls or on the partition wall between the living and service rooms.

The double-pile house was the ultimate development in house design at the vernacular level, providing a degree of comfort not found in earlier houses. The plan, modified to make a feature of the central hallway and staircase, became increasingly popular during the eighteenth century, with the rise of brick building, and remained so until the late nineteenth century. In some instances features such as pilasters, cornices and arched heads, created from cut and rubbed bricks, were introduced. Combinations of colours produced by different degrees of firing were also used to give decorative effect.

Priests' Houses

The idea that every priest should have a house and land originated at the Lateran Council of 1215, when the Pope ordered that a reasonable living, with secure tenure, be provided for them. There was a wide variation in the status and income of these priests, and those houses that have survived are not probably typical of the majority; some would have corresponded to those of the yeoman farmers, many would have been little more than humble cottages.

Before the Reformation most parish priests were celibate and, from the evidence available, separate accommodation was provided for a resident housekeeper or servant, generally with no direct access to the rest of the house. In addition these medieval priests' houses had to serve other needs, such as providing hospitality for travellers, so guest rooms were also required. After the Reformation it was not uncommon for the priest to marry and the provision of a study seems to have been an important feature. These early priests' houses would not have been distinguishable from the majority of farmhouses in the village, and it was not until later, in the eighteenth and nineteenth centuries, that the greater wealth and higher status of some of the clergy led to the construction of many of the large Georgian rectories that can be seen today.

Most medieval priests' houses were situated either within or

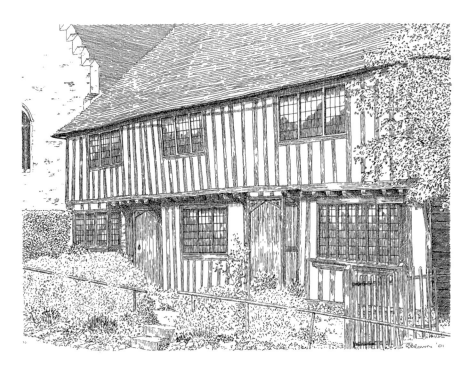

90 *Priest's house, Smallhythe, Kent*

overlooking the churchyard. A great many villages contain so-called priests' houses but it is not always clear that this was their original purpose. The priest's house at Smallhythe in Kent is an example of one rebuilt after a fire of 1516 which destroyed the village and church. A few date from before the Reformation, the most famous of these being the early timber-framed clergy house at Alfriston, East Sussex, which was built for a small community of parish priests around 1350. After the Reformation it became the vicarage of St Andrew's Church until about 1790, when it was converted into two farm labourers' cottages. The building became derelict in the 1880s and was acquired by the National Trust in 1896 at a cost of £10, becoming the first building and the second property to come into their care.

Another early priest's house, also owned by the National Trust, is to be found at Easton on the Hill, Northamptonshire. Although the precise date of its construction is unknown, architectural evidence points to the early sixteenth century. The moulded timber beams, however, appear to date from around 1400 and are likely to have been reused from an earlier building. Almost nothing is known of its early

91 *Clergy house, Alfriston, East Sussex*

history but the building would have been designed for a pre-Reformation celibate priest. In about 1690 the new rectory was built next door and the Old Rectory, as it became known, was probably used to house Garford School, set up by the Garford Charity to educate the poor children of the parish. How long it was used as a school is unknown but by 1852 the outbuildings, of which the Old Rectory formed part, were described as barns and stables. In 1867 extensive repairs were carried out, the external stairway was removed and a pitching door was provided on the first floor behind the fireplace. For almost a century the upper floor was used as a hayloft, with pigs and cattle below. In 1963 the building was in a poor condition and to prevent its demolition it was purchased by the National Trust and repaired, the lower floor becoming a village meeting room and the

92 *Priest's house, Easton on the Hill, Northamptonshire*

upper floor a museum of bygones. The building was again extensively repaired in 1984–5.

Other notable examples of priests' houses include the one at Martock in Somerset, which was built by the Treasurers of Wells Cathedral, a stone fifteenth-century one at Muchelney in Somerset and one at West Hoathly in West Sussex. This is a particularly interesting building, being of timber construction with wattle and daub infilling and with a splendid Horsham stone slate roof. The property was originally owned by the great Cluniac Priory of St Pancras at Lewes which, in 1391, obtained permission from the Pope to appropriate the 'rectory' of West Hoathly, appointing a vicar to serve the church and other parishes. In 1524 the house was let by the priory to a tenant farmer and in 1538 it was seized by Henry VIII and soon afterwards given to his secretary, Thomas Cromwell, and, on his execution in 1540, to Anne of Cleves. Later it passed to Queen Elizabeth, who sold it around 1560. It was at this time that a chimney and floor were inserted into the open hall. In the 1960s it was saved for posterity by a John King.

93 *Priest's house, Muchelney, Somerset*

94 *Priest's house, West Hoathly, West Sussex*

Cottages

The majority of houses in villages are these days termed as cottages but true cottages, which were built for the landless labouring classes, are rare before the middle of the eighteenth century. Any built earlier than this would have been insubstantial, and would rarely have survived a generation or two before they needed rebuilding. So the majority of so-called cottages dating from before around 1750 would have started out as the houses of people of some means.

As early as the fifteenth and sixteenth centuries, as the farmers abandoned their village homes for more spacious houses on their newly acquired lands, the old buildings within the village were often divided into tenements. Former hall and cross-passage houses were often divided into three, the upper end, containing the parlour, forming one unit, the hall another and the service rooms the third. Typical of this process is Old Court Cottage, Limpsfield, Surrey, originally the court-house of the Abbot of Battle's outlying manor at Limpsfield, which was used as an administrative unit from which the Abbot's feudal interests were supervised. Of aisled construction it was built, it is suggested, around 1200 and when the manor was let it was converted to a typical farmhouse by the removal of the aisles and the insertion of a new partition to form a cross-passage and service bays. Later it was converted into three humble cottages. Piecemeal alterations and additions over the centuries have sometimes so transformed some houses that their original identity has been lost.

Many of today's cottages, built before the eighteenth century, would formerly have belonged to small farmers, tradesmen and craftsmen, such as blacksmiths and wheelwrights, who were well enough off to own a cottage but seldom wealthy enough to indulge in great displays of grandeur. Their homes would have been small, probably no more than two ground-floor rooms and rarely two storeys high, with access to the attic by means of a ladder.

From Tudor times onwards there was an ever-increasing number of landless labourers, many of whom had lost their small parcel of land through enclosures. Large-scale enclosure schemes, with the backing of Acts of Parliament, were undertaken from the middle of the eighteenth century until the latter part of the nineteenth century, not only

95 *Old Court Cottage, Limpsfield, Surrey*

enclosing the open fields but also great tracts of unimproved common land, often to the further impoverishment of small farmers. Landless labourers were forced to build humble cottages on roadside verges or on small parcels of common land at the margins of the village which survived enclosure.

Most of these would soon have disappeared but a few survived long enough to gain a foothold, being improved upon with more durable materials, and lasting to the present time. Many would have been mean, one-roomed houses built of timber, mud or stone. One which survives is Chestnut Cottage at Clavering in Essex, which is typical. Dating from the seventeenth century it originally had a single room measuring 10 by 8 feet (3 by 2.4 metres). The cottage known as Toy Cottage at Church Lench, Worcestershire, is said to have once housed a family of fourteen.

Similar cottages can be found at Exton in Rutland (stone), and Gilmorton and Diseworth in Leicestershire (mud and timber respectively). At Ketton, also in Rutland, is a stone single-cell house dated 1629. The single room would have contained only a hearth or fireplace situated on the rear wall or, more commonly, on the gable wall. Often there was no ceiling, except perhaps at one end where there was a kind of loft reached by a ladder. Where the upper floor extended throughout, the space was lit by a dormer window or a window to the gable wall. Access to this area was by a ladder, a straight flight of steps or newel stairs located in one corner.

96 *Chestnut Cottage, Clavering, Essex*

Single-storey cottages were a feature in some parts, particularly in those areas associated with mining and quarrying, and in many remote moorland areas they are an important element of the rural scene. The accommodation was contained within a single structural cell, often divided into two, the whole open to the roof except that sometimes, there might have been a loose floor over the smaller room.

In closed villages, those with a single landowner, acceptable

97 *Toy Cottage, Church Lench, Worcestershire*

housing was often provided, although the quality varied considerably. Many landowners who provided new houses had ulterior motives, often destroying the old village to create a new one away from his newly erected mansion, as we have seen. Others were built to form part of the

landscape, incorporating all the elements of the romantic cottage advo-
cated by the Picturesque movement. However, many others built with
more philanthropic motives. In the open villages, where there was no
dominant landlord, rows of cottages were sometimes erected by local
tradesmen, who relied on large groups for their livelihood. Among the
earliest rows were the one at Boxworth in Cambridgeshire, which dates
from the first half of the eighteenth century. Most, however, date from
the end of that century, like a row at Bletchingdon, Oxfordshire, dated
1794, and another at Litlington in Cambridgeshire.

In many areas there was little incentive to provide housing, for the
wages were so low that few tenants could afford to pay an economic
rent. This remained the position until well into the nineteenth century,
when the failure of speculative development to meet the social needs of
the community forced many farmers to build cottages to house their
workers. This corresponded with the availability of material from further
afield for the first time, with the improvement in roads, railways and
canals, and led to the decline of the vernacular tradition. Brick became
the dominant material, Welsh slates began to replace tiles, stone slates
and thatch throughout the country, for they were cheap and light,
requiring only a lightly constructed roof. New, improved methods of
producing larger panes of glass allowed for bigger windows, which gave
more light and air to the rooms. Earthen floors were replaced with brick
or stone flags, panelled doors replaced old boarded ones. House
construction therefore became cheaper and many of our village cottages
date from this period – the last half of the nineteenth century.

Small, poorly constructed cottages continued to be built and old
farm buildings converted into dwellings, but more substantial cottages
now also began to appear. Simple one-up, one-down, or two-up, two-
down, cottages, built either in pairs or in terraces, became common.
The arrangement within each cottage was simple: the largest room
always had a fireplace on one of the gable walls, with the second room
either alongside the main room or behind it. On the upper floor, which
was reached by a staircase which was usually placed next to the stack or
between the rooms, were two bedrooms, interconnected, for there was
rarely independent access from a landing. Single-storeyed outbuildings
were often placed at the rear of the house. Sometimes the cottages,
instead of being built next to each other, were back to back. Bay
windows, either on the ground floor or on both floors, became a
feature in many of them.

Pattern books appeared in ever-increasing numbers to help the would-be-builder, but what was built did not always match these designs. The more architecturally ambitious built cottages which showed the influence of the Picturesque, but these designs were often condemned as being impracticable.

Public health legislation improved housing conditions but did nothing to ease the increasing shortage of accommodation for the working man and his family. By the beginning of the twentieth century cottage building had fallen to a very low level, for agriculture was in depression and investment in rural housing was regarded as unprofitable. It was finally left to local authorities to provide the necessary housing for the rural workers.

Occupational Houses

Industry has always been part of rural life and up until the Industrial Revolution much of it would have been carried out in people's houses. These cottage industries were varied and widespread and many cottages were adapted or built to suit their requirements.

Textile work in its various forms was one of the principal rural cottage industries. It was Edward III who persuaded Flemish cloth workers to emigrate to England, and many settled in south-east and eastern England, the Pennines and the Cotswolds, where wool was readily available. In these areas – and elsewhere – weavers' cottages and clothiers' houses are to be found. There are fine examples of early weavers' cottages that can be found at Kersey and Water Street, Lavenham, both in Suffolk, and near the church at Goudhurst in Kent.

Although the woollen industry was in decline by the beginning of the eighteenth century in the south-east and East Anglia, elsewhere other industries such as some cotton processes, lace-making and hosiery all continued to flourish as cottage industries until well into the nineteenth century. Many cottages used in these industries can be seen in parts of Yorkshire, Lancashire, Nottinghamshire, Leicestershire and elsewhere. Plenty of light was needed and additional windows were often added to domestic premises, as at Sutton Bonington, Nottinghamshire, where a timber-framed cottage in Soar Lane, dated

98 *Weavers' cottages, Kersey, Suffolk*

1661, had long windows on the first floor inserted in the eighteenth century. Later purpose-built houses incorporating small frame-shops on the top floor were built, as at Stapleford, Nottinghamshire, or on the ground floor and running the whole depth of the house, as at Earl Shilton, Leicestershire and Calverton, Nottinghamshire, were built.

Similar properties are to be found in many of the villages of the Pennines. One of the most notable is Heptonstall, West Yorkshire, a centre of the handloom weaving trade, with its own Cloth Hall dating from 1568, where the weavers took their goods to be sold and which in its heyday rivalled the famous Piece Hall in Halifax. In Lancashire, in the foothills of the Pennines around Saddleworth Moor similar weavers' cottages are to be found in places like Greenfield, Greater Manchester. Here there is a fine example of a domestic weaving settlement which at one time provided accommodation for as many as seven families. Known as Higher Kinders, it dates from the early part of the seventeenth century, and the little group of buildings displays

99 *Cottage at Sutton Bonington, Nottinghamshire*

100 *Weavers' houses, Heptonstall, West Yorkshire*

many features associated with the domestic woollen industry, including the 'take-in' steps, which led up to a workroom extending the full length of the house, as well as long mullioned windows to provide maximum light. Close by is a small building which functioned as a dyehouse and here one can find the 'wuzzing holes' which were used in the drying of raw wool or weft. The process involved removing the excess water from the wool by being 'wuzzed' around in a basket slung from a pole, one end of which was inserted in the hole.

101 *Higher Kinders, Saddleworth, Greater Manchester*

Cottages similar to those in Nottinghamshire and Leicestershire are also found in northern Northamptonshire and southern Leicestershire. They were built for the boot and shoe industry, which remained a domestic industry longer than those related to textiles, even in some cases taking over the latter's premises.

With the coming of turnpike roads, canals and railways new types of occupational houses appeared. It was in 1663 that the first turnpike road appeared between Wadesmill in Herefordshire and Stilton in Cambridgeshire, and by 1800 there were some 1,100 turnpike trusts controlling around 23,000 miles (34,800 km) of road. These trusts were responsible for the upkeep of the roads which passed through their parishes. Gates were erected and tollhouses were built to collect the tolls. A variety of styles can still be seen around the country despite road improvement schemes, which have led to many being destroyed. They are usually facetted, or even round, to enable windows to face in both directions along the road so that the tollkeeper could observe traffic and open the gate, which adjoined the house, to collect the

102 *Guard house, Baslow, Derbyshire*

tolls. Tolls were also charged for the use of bridges, and there are still some reminders of this practice. At Baslow in Derbyshire there is a most unusual structure, a small guard house which was used in the collection of tolls for crossing the bridge. No record of the tolls charged exists; the only surviving record is a decree of 1500 as to what may not pass over the bridge: 'No one shall henceforth lead or carry any millstones over the bridge to Basselowe under the pain of 6/8d.'

With the coming of the canals, houses were provided for lock-keepers. They were normally designed by the canal's architect and were therefore distinctive to each canal. Tolls were also collected on the canals and agents' houses with special offices erected to collect them. A good example is to be found at Kirk Hallam in Derbyshire.

In the Cotswolds one finds, as part of the network of the Thames Severn Canal, a number of unusual roundhouses built for canal workers whose responsibility was to act as watchmen and maintain the canal in good repair. One example stands at Chalford, Gloucestershire. Built in 1798 it is now used as a studio for craftsmen.

Like lock-keepers' houses, houses and cottages for stationmasters and level-crossing keepers were also constructed by the railways' own architects and there are distinctive patterns for each railway. With the introduction of automatic level-crossing barriers, however, many of the cottages have disappeared.

FIVE

Public Buildings

For centuries the Church, especially the monasteries, provided for the educational needs of the village, as well as for the poor and needy. With the Dissolution of the Monasteries greater responsibility began to fall into secular hands. Public buildings began to appear in our villages to provide for their educational and institutional needs, in addition to semi-public ones which provided a service to the community.

Market Crosses and Halls

The right to hold a weekly market or annual fair was granted to a medieval town corporation or lord of the manor by royal charter. Between 1198 and 1483 some 2,400 grants were made, over half of them before 1275. The manorial lord found the market profitable, as he was able to extract tolls from stallholders as well a selling his surplus goods. The royal charter frequently specified the day on which the market or fair was to be held so that it did not coincide with any other local market.

We have seen that many churchyard crosses, in addition to their religious functions, were also used for commercial transactions. Similar in design to these were market crosses, which were placed in the centre of the market and, like churchyard crosses probably had a variety of uses, not only providing a focal point from which the traders and inhabitants could be addressed, but also a point at which tolls could be paid and business transactions undertaken.

Early medieval crosses had a stepped base and a shaft with a decorative head, but today few remain intact for, like the church-yard crosses, many were destroyed after the Reformation and all that now remains are the steps and a broken cross. Some, however, have survived or been restored; at Brigstock, Northamptonshire, the cross stands in the former market square, indicating the importance of one of the largest villages in the Royal Forest of Rockingham. Erected in the reign of Elizabeth, its head may have been reworked from a medieval cross. Another at Lavenham, Suffolk, erected in 1502, still stands in the centre of the market square.

103 *Market cross, Brigstock, Northamptonshire*

Not all market crosses are of this type; there are a few which, for some reason, have an uncon-ventional design. The butter cross, which stands on the green of the lovely Leicestershire village of Hallaton, is one example. It is a solid, circular structure with a conical roof. Another which is somewhat out of the ordinary is the one at Norham, Northumberland, but here only the base is medieval for the top did not survive, and the present upper part dates from only 1870.

105 *Market cross, Cheddar, Somerset*

104 *Market cross, Lavenham, Suffolk*

It soon became apparent that to provide protection for traders and toll collectors, some sort of cover was required. In many instances a roof was built around the cross, supported on stone or timber pillars. One of the finest is to be found at Castle Combe, Wiltshire, often described as England's most picturesque village.

At Cheddar in Somerset the old cross was built in the usual manner with a stepped base, shaft and decorative head, and was surrounded,

106 *Butter cross, Abbots Bromley, Staffordshire*

107 *Butter cross, Harrold, Bedfordshire*

probably in the seventeenth century, by an hexagonal structure with open four-centred arches. It was extensively restored in 1887.

In some instances there was no cross, and the structure comprised only an open framework of pillars supporting the roof, although a cross might surmount the roof as a symbol. These are often of timber construction. In other instances the vestige of a cross might have been retained in the form of a central pillar whose main function was to support the roof. The butter cross at Abbots Bromley, Staffordshire, is one such example and is a reminder of the days when Abbots Bromley was a market town. The hexagonal, pyramid-roofed timber-framed building stands at the edge of the village green and, although its central post states that the butter cross was probably built in 1339, it seems more likely that the present structure was erected some 300 years later. In other places the central pillar was abandoned leaving an open space for the traders. At Harrold, Bedfordshire, there is a typical example on the village green. For many years the village had a flourishing cottage industry in lace-making.

The last stage in the development of these structures was the addition of an upper storey, to house the traders' guild, the toll collector or even the parish council. A fine example stands in the main street at Winster, Derbyshire. It is the most dominant feature of the village and

108 *Market house, Winster, Derbyshire*

stands as testimony to the village's once thriving past. At the beginning of the eighteenth century, Winster had a population probably in excess of 2,000. Lead mining was the principal means of employment and as the village grew so too did other trades and services. In 1711 a grant was made for the holding of a fair and it was around this time that the market house is thought to have been constructed; it became a focal

109 *Market cross, Tickhill, South Yorkshire*

point of the village. It followed the traditional pattern of such buildings, two storeys high, originally with an open ground floor and the
upper storey supported on arches. The date at which these arches were
filled in is not known. The ground floor was used by merchants and
miners to weigh out the lead, while in the upper storey, poultry, eggs
and butter were traded. Towards the end of the eighteenth century the
demand for lead dwindled and Winster became less prosperous. The
Fair, which had been so important, became less so and the market
house was neglected. By the end of the nineteenth century it was in a
ruinous condition and in 1904 the upper floor had to be removed for
safety reasons. In 1906, however, it was acquired by the National Trust,
who restored it, wherever possible using the old materials. Today it is
used by the Trust as an information centre.

Another memorable example is at Dunster, Somerset – the yarn
market, built in the late sixteenth century and subsequently restored. It
is a complete hexagonal timber-framed structure carrying a large roof
covered with stone slates.

Market crosses continued to be built well into the eighteenth century,
often replacing earlier ones, but still retaining the medieval concept of an
open ground floor. Now, however, the design was Classical, taking the
form of a rotunda supported on stone columns. These are found in small
market towns, such as Swaffham in Norfolk and Bungay in Suffolk.
Another stands in the market place at Mountsorrel, Leicestershire, once
a market town and an eighteenth-century centre of the hosiery trade but
today only a village. The market cross, a domed rotunda on eight Tuscan
columns, was built in 1793 by William Thomas for Sir John Danvers,
who took the medieval cross to Swithland Hall. A similar one stands in
the village of Tickhill in South Yorkshire.

Guildhalls

Former guildhalls can be found in many of our villages, primarily in
eastern England but also elsewhere, for instance in the attractive hamlet of
Stoford, Somerset, which had a 'Zuldhous' in 1353, although the present
building dates from the sixteenth century. The majority were built for religious guilds, formed of lay people who paid a subscription and left

110 *Guildhall, Stoford, Somerset*

bequests 'for the assistance of brethren in distress in times of sickness and want'. In many cases these guilds provided money to offset the costs of funerals for its members. In addition, prayers and obits, or anniversary masses, were said regularly on behalf of its members, both living and dead.

These fraternities, being of a religious and social nature, frequently sited their halls close to the village church, often at the edge of the churchyard. Although many of these religious guilds are of great antiquity, their guildhalls are rarely so old. The majority are of fifteenth or early sixteenth-century date, probably reflecting the increased wealth during this period.

Religious guilds were suppressed following the Charities Act of 1547, when there was a general dissolution of charities that had endowments involving prayers for the dead. Their property was confiscated by the Crown and later sold by the Court of Augmentations for secular use. Some guildhalls were used by the villages as meeting places; others were divided into tenements, or into shops or workshops for local traders and craftsmen; others still were used as schools. Many more became parish workhouses and almshouses.

In eastern England the surviving guildhalls are timber-framed, the most common form being a long, relatively narrow building, generally of two storeys and jettied along the front and often at one end. The upper floor, where the guild met, was generally one single room, although sometimes it was divided into two – one large room which could accommodate all the members and a small antechamber which might incorporate a service room or perhaps a kitchen. Access to the upper floor was often gained by means of an external staircase to the rear or at the end. The ground floor was usually divided into a number of small rooms whose use is now not clear. They may have been used by the guilds as small meeting places, but there is evidence that some were used as shops, perhaps to provide the guild with additional income. At Finchingfield, Essex, the ground floor seems to have been used from the beginning as almshouses, which remained in occupation until about 1930; they have now been converted into accommodation for the elderly.

There are many fine examples of guildhalls. At Stoke-by-Nayland, Suffolk, across the road from the lych-gate, is a magnificent timber-framed building built in the early fifteenth century as a meeting place for the village's religious guilds. According to Westlake's *Parish Gilds of Medieval England*, Stoke-by-Nayland had four guilds, St John the Baptist, St Peter the Apostle, Holy Trinity and Our Lady, each of which used the guildhall. It comprised one large room on the upper floor jettied to the front and north end. Inside, the magnificent roof, which includes alternate hammer-beams and arched braces, indicates the great wealth of those guilds. The room was reached by way of a stair tower to the rear. The ground floor comprised a number of rooms and there is evidence of a shop in the centre. Towards the southern end of the building there appears to have been an archway through it. In 1619 it became the parish workhouse and it was at this time that the large brick chimney was inserted. It remained the village

111 *Guildhall, Stoke-by-Nayland, Suffolk*

workhouse until 1834, when the new Poor Laws were introduced. Later it was converted into three cottages and is now under covenant to the National Trust.

In addition to these religious guildhalls there were others belonging to guilds concerned with a trade or craft or group of allied trades. These were found mainly in towns. Perhaps the most famous is the one at Thaxted, Essex, built for the Guild of Cutlers early in the fifteenth century, with an open ground floor which was undoubtedly used for trading, thus combining the guild's requirements with those of the market hall.

Although these were primarily trade guilds, religion often played an important part in their affairs. The famous half-timbered guildhall at Lavenham, Suffolk, was built in about 1528 by the Guild of Corpus Christi, one of three guilds in the town to regulate the wool trade. Religious festivals were always celebrated with processions through the streets from the guildhall to the church, and religious feasts were held in the hall. After 1547 the guildhall was used only for secular purposes. It was used to regulate a much-reduced wool trade before becoming parish property in 1596. It was used as the town hall for nearly eighty years, after which it became first a prison, then a workhouse, then, with the adjoining cottages, almshouses and finally a wool store. By the 1880s it was in poor repair and was purchased in 1887 by Sir Cuthbert Quilter, who undertook the repairs. It is now owned by the National Trust and is open to the public.

In 1835 the legal powers of the trade guilds were ended, but long before this they had been in decline, owing in part to state control, and in part to the rise of new industries.

Church Houses

We have seen that the medieval church not only served the village through its primary purpose of religious worship, but was also the focus of social life in the village. Parish feasts, known as church-ales, were held regularly, especially on the patronal festival of the church and at Whitsun, Midsummer and Michaelmas. Ale and food were sold and entertainment provided, and churchwardens' accounts provide evidence of the effectiveness of these functions in providing money for church funds, as well as for the benefit of the poor of the village. These activities were in many cases held in the nave of the church, which, up until the sixteenth century, would have been an open area free of pews. However, by the beginning of that century the use of the church for such activities began to be frowned upon by the church authorities, especially after the Act of 1571 forbade the use of the church itself for feasting. Church houses now began to appear. Built near to or adjoining the churchyard, the church house was the predecessor of the village hall, sometimes also providing living accommodation for the clergy. It occurs, for some reason, mainly in the eastern and south-western counties.

In the West Country most church houses appear to date from the first half of the sixteenth century and are generally two-storeyed, often of ashlar, with an external staircase leading to a single room on the upper floor. G.W. Copland identified over sixty survivors in Devon alone, of which those at Holcombe Rogus, Throwleigh, South Tawton and Winkleigh – the latter built in 1535 at a cost of £24 14s 4d – are the most notable. The grandest in the county, however, is at Widecombe in the Moor, and was built of granite ashlar in 1537. Unique in having a loggia with seven octagonal columns, it was originally for people from outlying parts to rest before the church service. Church-ales were served there and continued until the seventeenth century. In the nineteenth century the ground floor was used as almshouses, whilst the upper floor was used for the village school. The National Trust acquired the building in 1933, and that part of the house known as Sexton's Cottage is used by the Trust as an information centre; the rest is leased as a village hall.

The church house which adjoins the churchyard at Cheriton Fitzpaine, Devon, is one of the most picturesque. Built of cob, it has a thatched roof which is claimed to be the largest thatched roof in England on a purpose-built building as opposed to a row of cottages or barns. The building dates from the sixteenth century. By 1648 a 'school chamber' had been established and in 1754 this, together with the remainder of the building, which had long been an unregulated poorhouse, had become the parish workhouse. By 1850 it had become the parish school which it still is today.

Somerset, too, has some good examples of church houses. The one at Crowcombe was built in 1481, £12 2s 11d being paid to the masons and carpenters for their labour and materials out of church funds. The one at

112 *Church house, South Tawton, Devon*

Crowcombe was given to the parish in 1515 and, like others, is two-storeyed, with the meeting hall on the first floor reached by external stairs, the rooms on the ground floor being used as a kitchen and for storage. In 1668 Elizabeth Carew left £200 to the parish and 33 acres (13.4 ha) of land was purchased in nearby Bishops Lydeard, the rent being sufficient to teach fifteen poor boys 'to read, write and cast sums, the boys to have annually a suit of plain clothes' and to pay the master's salary. The upper storey was used as the village school until the present school was built in 1872. The ground floor accommodated the village poor until they were moved to the dreaded workhouse at Williton, which was erected in 1837. By 1907 the building was said to be 'quite ruinous', but an appeal raised £550 for the necessary repairs. Today the lower part is being used as the village hall, and the upper floor for regular craft and art exhibitions. The one at Chew Magna was built in about 1510, and is today used as a museum. In Gloucestershire the finest example perhaps is the one at Standish, which dates from the sixteenth century and overlooks the churchyard.

Whereas church houses in south-west England were of stone, in the eastern counties they were timber-framed. In 1527 one was built 'at a common charge of the Townshippe' at Landbeach, Cambridgeshire, for church-ales and parish meetings.

Following the suppression of the guilds in 1547, when guildhalls became parish property, many became church houses; the large first floor provided the accommodation required for celebrating parish festivals and holidays. The former guildhalls at Fressingfield, Cockfield and Yoxford, all in Suffolk, became church houses.

After the Reformation church-ales were frowned upon by both the Puritans and the magistracy and church houses gradually began to disappear, and with them the custom of church-ales. Some became alehouses, like the Fox and Goose Inn, Fressingfield, and the Greyhound Inn, Pettistree, both in Suffolk, and the Fleur-de-Lis, Stoke sub Hamdon, Somerset, which was probably built in 1544 and converted to an inn by the eighteenth century. Others became the property of the parish and many in the seventeenth century were converted into poorhouses, while others became schools. Many, like those at Walkhampton, Devon, and Cockfield and Yoxford, Suffolk, have now been converted into dwellings.

Town Halls and Courthouses

A few villages have town halls – an indication of their former importance. In construction and layout many of the early examples closely resemble market halls in that the ground floor was open, with the upper floor supported on columns. One such example is to be found at Fordwich in Kent, the former port to Canterbury. Built, it is believed, shortly before 1544, it had a courtroom and jury room on the first floor, with the ground floor open; the latter was later enclosed to form a storeroom and lock-up. The building is most attractive. It is jettied on all four sides and the upper floor is filled in with herringbone brick nogging beneath a large hipped roof. It is reputed to be the smallest town hall in the country. Another which makes this claim is at Corfe Castle, Dorset, which was built in 1770 with a council chamber on the first floor approached from the side, and lock-up cells on the ground floor. These now form a museum of ball clay working, quarrying and country crafts.

Chipping Campden, Gloucestershire, is perhaps one of the finest examples of a town which has declined in importance over the centuries, and is now no more than a large village. In the Middle Ages it was an important centre for collecting and despatching wool, England's chief export. It had a weekly market and annual fair as early as 1274. The Revd. F.E. Witts, the 'Cotswold Parson', wrote in 1836: 'Campden is a

113 *Town hall, Newtown, Isle of Wight*

dull, clean, disused market town. In former times of greater prosperity it was the seat of an active trade in woollen cloths; but those days and that trade have long since passed away.' All that remains of its former importance is the market hall, numerous important houses and, situated in Market Place, the town hall. Of fourteenth century origin, it still retains two buttresses of this period with traceried panels. It was largely rebuilt, however, early in the nineteenth century.

Newtown on the Isle of Wight was chartered in 1256, but the town failed and now it is a mere handful of houses, with traces of a street grid. The town hall, built in the late seventeenth century, was an attempt to revive the town but with no effect. It is the only remaining symbol of Newtown's former eminence – it once returned two members of parliament, but the Reform Act of 1832 declared the place a rotten borough and ended its parliamentary status. In the early years of the last century the building was in a poor state, but in 1933 an anonymous group of benefactors, calling themselves Ferguson's Gang, purchased it, restored it, and gave it to the National Trust.

The town hall at Clun, Shropshire, was built in 1780, when it was a busy market town, but in the twentieth century it has declined to village status. The town hall was constructed by 2nd Lord Clive, using stone from the courthouse which stood near the castle.

Courthouses were once also prominent features of some villages. In medieval England manorial courts were held in the open hall of the manor house, presided over either by the lord of the manor or, more likely, one of his stewards. The little fifteenth-century courthouse at Hawkshead, Cumbria, is the only surviving part of the large manor house which was owned by the monks of Furness Abbey. When the manorial system declined other buildings were found in which to administer local justice. We have seen that town halls often doubled as courthouses but, in some cases, other buildings were provided. The village of Milton Regis in Kent was once larger than nearby Sittingbourne, which has now almost engulfed it. Its former importance is indicated by the free-standing, timber-framed courthouse in the main street. It has been dated to the early part of the fifteenth century but became derelict and was restored in the 1960s. It has a hipped roof and a continuous overhang to the east side only, and the gratings of the two lock-ups look towards the street.

Near the church at Long Crendon, Buckinghamshire, stands a four-teenth-century building with a timber upper storey, most of which comprises one long room. It was originally used as a staple hall or wool

114 *Courthouse, Long Crendon, Buckinghamshire*

115 *Courthouse, Pevensey, East Sussex*

store but later became a courthouse, and manorial courts were held there in the fifteenth century by the stewards of Catherine, wife of Henry V, who owned the manor. In 1900 the courthouse was one of the first buildings acquired by the National Trust. Sometimes a lock-up formed an integral part of a courthouse as at Pevensey, East Sussex.

In many cases a room in the local inn was often used as a courthouse; one such was the New Inn, Pembridge, Herefordshire, which originated as a farmhouse in 1311 and was much enlarged with matching gable wings in the seventeenth century, with the cellar being used as a dungeon. The Bear Inn, Bisley, Gloucestershire, is another inn which was once used as a courthouse; the old village lock-up, dated 1824, is nearby. The Castle Inn, Lydford, Devon, and the Punchbowl Inn, Lanreath,

116 *The Bear Inn, Bisley, Gloucestershire*

Cornwall, are other examples. The old courtroom at the Hark to Bounty at Slaidburn, Lancashire, still retains its original furnishings of oak benches, a dock and a witness box.

Hospitals and Almshouses

The medieval hospital, of which the modern version is its specialized successor, played an important role in the social life of England. Originally, as the name implies, it was a guesthouse in which poor travellers, as well as the sick and the old, could find shelter. They were also called maisons-dieu and later bedehouses and almshouses. They are to be found in all our principal cities and towns, as well as in many smaller towns and villages.

The idea of hospitals as independent institutions was already established in Saxon times. Many were founded by prominent churchmen, others by wealthy benefactors, still others by religious and craft guilds. Although a great many classes, such as discharged soldiers and sailors, decayed gentlefolk, and the widows of clergy, benefited from these institutions, the majority helped those in need who lived in the neighbourhood.

These hospitals were designed to provide not only for the material needs of the inmates but also for their spiritual requirements and so their plan usually comprised a large aisled hall, called the infirmary hall, with a chapel at its east end. The aisles, it seems, provided accommodation for rows of beds and were often divided into cubicles, with the centre of the hall left free for daily use. An open screen separated the chapel from the hall. St Mary's Hospital, Chichester, which was founded in the early thirteenth century but rebuilt at the end of the same century, is the finest example of this simple plan. When originally built, the hall measured 100 by 45 feet (30 by 14 metres), but this has been reduced in length by a third. The original cubicles have disappeared and were replaced, in the seventeenth century, by larger rooms, each with a tall chimney. The elaborate stone chapel has an arched opening into the hall, with an oak screen and stalls. It still functions as a charitable building after some 700 years.

This type of hospital was generally built in major towns but the aisled hall with a chancel to the east end has a certain resemblance to a parish church. It has been suggested by Walter H. Godfrey, in his book *The English Almshouse*, that the church at Westham, East Sussex, which stands outside the west gate at Pevensey, originated as an aisleless twelfth-century infirmary hall. Later, he suggests, it was reduced in length and a tower added to the west end, superseding the church at Peelings when the hamlet of Westham grew outside the gates of Pevensey.

The Reformation brought the end of the hospital with its infirmary hall and chapel, for both Henry VIII and Edward VI dissolved most of the old institutions on the pretext that the inmates were required to pray for the souls of the founders. However, poverty remained and, in accordance with a law passed during the reign of Elizabeth I to provide 'hospitals, bidings or working houses for the poor', many hospitals were re-established on secular lines. New benefactors, encouraged by their example, formed new establishments which we now know as almshouses, the inmates of which were carefully selected for their unquestionable virtue.

For the first time almshouses began to appear outside the large towns. One of the first, a pre-Reformation example, is the quadrangular set of almshouses at Ewelme, Oxfordshire, which was founded in 1437 by William de la Pole, Earl and afterwards Duke of Suffolk and his wife Alice to house thirteen poor men under the care of two chaplains. It is one of the earliest examples of an almshouse built on a collegiate plan, with a timber-framed cloister around a paved courtyard. The almshouses themselves are good examples of fifteenth-century timber-framed construction, with herringbone brick nogging to the courtyard. The group was originally thatched but is now tiled. The almshouses stand in the shadow of the west tower of the church, also built by the Duchess of Suffolk, and further down the hill are the schoolmaster's house and the schoolhouse, all forming a delightful group.

In some instances existing buildings were adapted to form new almshouses. One such was the college of Cobham, Kent, originally founded in 1362 to house six chantry priests. In 1598 William Brooke, 10th Lord Cobham, adapted and extended it to form the present building, with twenty almsfolks' apartments, accommodation for two wardens and a common hall, all around a quadrangle.

117 *Almshouse, Cobham, Kent*

Another adaptation is the bedehouse at Lyddington, Rutland, which originally belonged to the bishops of Lincoln. It was most likely built by Bishop Alnwick (1436–49) and altered by Bishops Russell (1480–94) and Smith (1496–1514). It was ceded by Henry VIII in 1547 and in 1602 came to Thomas, Lord Burghley. The present building is probably only one range of the original palace and was adapted by Lord Burghley to house a warden and twelve poor men and women.

The quadrangle became the standard form for almshouses at the beginning of the seventeenth century and many are of high architectural merit. In 1602 the Earl of Nottingham rebuilt the ancient hospital at Donnington, Berkshire, in the new Elizabethan style, with many brick gables and chimney stacks around a quadrangle. Twelve years later Henry Howard, Earl of Northampton, built a lovely gabled quadrangular hospital at Clun, Shropshire, for 'twelve poor men'.

118 *Bedehouse, Lyddington, Rutland*

An endowment made by the Duchess of Somerset resulted in the construction of Somerset Hospital at Froxfield in Wiltshire in 1694, a complete quadrangle of brick houses. Initially the group was built on a generous scale but the courtyard dimensions were doubled in 1775 while the entrance gate and Gothic revival stone chapel were added in 1813. The original design, closely followed by the eighteenth-century extension, was built in the local tradition of unadorned brickwork under a pitched tiled roof, the only embellishment being the two-light mullioned windows in stone – although wood was used in the 1775 extension.

The enclosed quadrangle was a marked feature of all types of buildings well into the eighteenth century, and it had a rival in the open quadrangle, in which one side was left unbuilt. An early example is at Etwall, Derbyshire, and was founded by Sir John Port in 1550, who also founded Repton School. The almshouses were rebuilt in 1681 but only the central front piece gives evidence of this date; the rest of this large, brick structure with stone dressings appears to be much older. To the south of the village is Etwall Lodge, built in 1812 for the master of the hospital. On a much smaller scale are the almshouses which Sir Stephen Soame endowed at Little Thurlow, Suffolk, in 1618, one year before his death. Built for nine poor people in three ranges facing a rectangular forecourt they are single-storeyed except for the gabled centre.

These examples apart, quadrangular almshouses are generally the province of towns; in villages most take the form of a single row of dwellings, often simple in their plan but with a great deal of character. There are numerous examples, generally dating from the beginning of the sixteenth century onwards, although a few are a little earlier.

At Long Melford, Suffolk, overlooking the green, is Trinity Hospital, built by Sir William Cordell in 1573 but much altered in 1847. Sir William, a lawyer and in turn Solicitor-General, Speaker of the House of Commons and Master of the Rolls, bought Melford Hall, which was originally owned by the abbots of Bury St Edmunds, after the Dissolution. The almshouses, which were founded for twelve men and two servants, are seven bays wide, with the first and last projecting as gable wings and a courtyard at the back overlooking the church and churchyard. The centre is embattled and has a cupola.

At East Coker, Somerset, is a charming row of stone cottages founded in 1640 by Archdeacon Helyar with a long series of gables with intervening chimney stacks. Archdeacon Helyar had been chaplain to Queen Elizabeth I and bought Coker Court from the Phelips family.

119 *Almshouses, East Coker, Somerset*

To the west of the church at St Germans in Cornwall is another remark-able row of almshouses in an unusually picturesque grouping. Built in 1583 by a member of the Moyle family to house twelve women, the building comprises two storeys, the six gables supported on plain stone piers with balconies above with wooden balustrades and a loggia on the ground floor. The balcony is reached by external stairs. The almswomen used to be presented at Christmas with a shilling and a sack of wheat, but now the gift takes the form of 2 pounds (900 grams) of beef. The building was reconstructed and reoccupied in 1967.

Attached to the north-west corner of the church at Wimborne St Giles, Dorset, is a row of single-storeyed almshouses forming an intriguing

120 *Almshouses, St Germans, Cornwall*

group overlooking a large open green at one of the entrances to St Giles House. They are built of soft red bricks with stone dressings. The only real elaboration occurs in the central bay, where a three-bay stone arcade leads through the building. Above the arcade is a fine armorial panel, a small oval in a brick panel and a gable on kneelers. This part is now open to the roof but was probably originally a first-floor chapel. They were built by Sir Anthony Ashley in 1624 as ten single-roomed tenements 'for the comfort in old age' of elderly widows from his estate.

A vigorous and flamboyant example is to be found at Crispe's Almshouses at Marshfield, Gloucestershire, which undoubtedly benefited from their proximity to the fine limestone quarries. Built in 1619 there are four units, each with a dormer in the traditional Cotswold style, on either side of a central porch, above which is a large gable incorporating

121 *Crispe's Almshouses, Marshfield, Gloucestershire*

122 *Hospital, Weekley, Northamptonshire*

a double panel with two boldly carved and florid hatchments in stone enclosed by a framework of three Classical columns with a base and entablature. Above the central gabled roof is a small tower with a spire marking the central chapel. The building remains externally substantially unaltered and still retains its two-light mullioned windows with wooden casements and a continuous string course at first-floor level and stepped hoodmoulds to the upper windows.

Another charming hospital built at around the same time, 1611, is to be found at Weekley, Northamptonshire. It was built by Sir Edward Montagu to house a master and six brethren, old retainers from his estate. The centrepiece of this otherwise simple building is somewhat capricious; obelisks abound, a favourite family motif, two on shells flanking the coat of arms and three at the bulbous shaped gable above. Between the coat of arms and the gable is a large painted sundial with the words *TEMPORA*

LABUNTUR TACITISQUE SENESCIMUS ANNIS – 'Time slips by and we grow old with silent years'. The hospital, no longer able to fulfil the intention of its owner, became a private house in 1972.

In 1665 Sir John Jacob constructed the almshouses in Church Street, Gamlingay, Cambridgeshire. Of brick, they are two-storeyed with two large and two small windows alternating on the upper floor. In the centre is an inscription panel with a coat of arms above flanked by two upright oval windows. In 1745 a chapel was added to the left of the building.

In 1681 Sir Stephen Fox built twelve brick almshouses at Farley, Wiltshire. They were arranged each side of a house for the warden and constructed, it seems, to the design of Sir Christopher Wren, who also designed the church. Sir Christopher's influence is to be seen in several almshouses of this period; at Stydd, Lancashire, there are five erected by the Shireburns in 1728 to house five Catholic widows. The building

123 *Almshouses, Stydd, Lancashire*

is of five bays; the three middle ones have, on the first floor, a three-bay arcade of rustic Tuscan columns.

There is no such Classical design at Quainton, Buckinghamshire, where, at the entrance to the churchyard, stand Winwood Almshouses, built in 1687 but still entirely in a pre-Classical style. They are single-storeyed, with dormers alternating between bigger and smaller gables and two porches, also with Dutch gables, each with the Winwood coat of arms in high relief. These almshouses reflect a style more suited to a village setting which remained in many secluded areas long after Classical styles had been established. It can also be seen in six almshouses erected in 1846 at Arrington, Cambridgeshire, by Susan, 4th Countess of Hardwicke, in memory of her mother. Constructed of red brick with stone dressings in the Tudor manner, they consist of a single-storeyed range fronting the road, with two-storeyed projecting wings, with a central gabled porch with a coat of arms above the door and two smaller porches at the angles of the front with the projecting wings. At the rear of the almshouses is a communal bakehouse. The building now belongs to the National Trust.

Poorhouses and Workhouses

Throughout the medieval period each parish was responsible for its poor; where the rectorial tithes were held by an ecclesiastical or monastic foundation, they obtained a proportion of that income for the relief of the poor. Following the Dissolution of the Monasteries the full responsibility fell on the parish and, although several acts were passed with regard to the gathering of charitable alms it was not until 1597 that parishes were able to levy a poor rate. In 1601 the Poor Law Act was passed authorizing parishes to build poorhouses for the incapacitated poor. It was as a result of this legislation that in some areas the first poorhouses were provided by the parish. A few would have built new dwellings, but many would have adapted other buildings.

As we have seen, many former guildhalls – for example Stoke-by-Nayland and Lavenham – and church houses – for example Chew Magna, Crowcombe and Cheriton Fitzpaine – were used to house the poor. Where no such building existed others were provided, as every parish owned a house or a few cottages which could be used to accommodate the poor. One such is Bridge House at Finchingfield, Essex, which dates from the sixteenth century and was, from 1767, used as the village workhouse for some thirty inmates. A contemporary description of conditions states: 'Old people and young children, ne'er-do-wells and imbeciles were all crowded together, the able-bodied paupers being let out to work in the hop grounds. The Master, a native of the parish, was a stern and much feared man who dressed in a kind of smock, with grey breeches and stockings and went in search of fugitives with a whip.' At Smarden, Kent, is Chessenden, a house originally built in 1462 and the finest Wealden house in the village, which was at one time the village workhouse. Another fifteenth-century Wealden house, which was used to house the village poor from 1684 until 1834, was Workhouse Cottages, on the edge of the village of Steyning, West Sussex.

In 1723 Knatchbull's General Workhouse Act empowered parishes, or groups of parishes, to build workhouses to house, feed and employ the ill, aged, orphaned and the general poor. In many cases these were large and often impressive buildings, frequently described as 'paupers' palaces' and built along domestic Georgian lines. Many, however, were built and maintained at minimum cost, and conditions were poor. Some had separate wards for the young, for the old, for men and for women. In Suffolk a number of 'houses of industry' were built from the mid 1760s to the mid 1780s; they were substantial, plain brick buildings of Classical composition but without too much unnecessary elaboration. Seven were built in total: those at Bulcamp, Shipmeadow, and Tattingstone were all begun in 1765, followed by ones at Barham, Melton and Semer (1780), and finally Onehouse, near Stowmarket (1777–81). The buildings were extensive, often of an H- or E-shaped plan, usually of brick and two-storeyed, with one of the wings often containing a chapel. At Tattingstone the buildings were enlarged in 1819 and again in 1837, forming three sides of a quadrangle, with, in the centre, a low apsed chapel, although this was not part of the original plan.

Similar buildings were built in Norfolk, such as those at Gressenhall and Hales. Gressenhall was built in 1776–7 on the site of an old farm, and was a large, plain brick building with a symmetrical façade, a central pediment and a rooftop cupola, with projecting wings at each end. Between 450 and 670 paupers lived there, the able-bodied working in the fields, others at weaving, spinning and domestic chores. There was

124 *Chessenden, Smarden, Kent*

education for the young. Although the working day was long there was no unnecessary discipline and the food, although dull, was plentiful.

After the 1834 Poor Law Amendment Act the more liberal conditions were abandoned and workhouses began to resemble prisons; a hard, primitive regime was introduced in order to reduce the expenses and keep all but the very poor away – poverty became almost a crime. New, grim workhouses were erected in the 1830s, often to designs by keen young architects like G.G. Scott and William Moffatt. A number still survive, of which Williton Union Workhouse, Somerset, which was built in 1838–40 to the design of Moffatt and later became known as Townsend House, ranks as one of the best and the most complete. The

T-shaped wings project from a central four-storeyed block for the wardens. Facing the street there is a handsome entrance archway with flanking public and visiting rooms. The subdued, Classical style suggests a respectable and comfortable establishment, which it was not.

A report in 1909 spelt the beginning of the end of the work-houses and in 1913 they became Poor Law Institutions, but the imagery and fear they evoked remained until the introduction of unemployment benefit in 1929. Many of the surviving workhouses were adapted for other uses, such as hospitals, like those at Bulcamp, Tattingstone and Williton. Now even these are being abandoned in preference to larger, centralized hospitals and their future is threat-ened again. Some have been adapted to provide housing, as at Tattingstone. The one at Gressenhall was converted to form the Museum of Rural Life, and some of the bleak atmosphere has been retained on purpose to reflect its past.

Schools

As the priest was frequently the only literate person in a village, it was often left to the Church to provide the first education, and it seems that in many cases the Church also provided the accommodation. This link between Church and education began in the Middle Ages and continued well into the nineteenth century. However, many of the schools were short-lived or intermittent, often depending upon the incumbent or curate or the presence of a suitably educated layman. There is documentary evidence that the chancel of the church was often used, or that part of one of the aisles was separated off, or that a chapel or the room above the porch was set aside. At Long Melford, Suffolk, the Lady Chapel was used as a 'Publick Schoole for Melford' in 1670 and a multiplication table which was used by the children still survives on the east wall. At Old Dilton, near Westbury, Wiltshire, the gallery in the north-east corner of the church, which has a separate entrance, was for a long time used as the village school. Similarly at Avebury in Wiltshire, the village school was held for a hundred years in the gallery in the south aisle. When lessons were not held in the village church, parish charity schoolrooms were built in the churchyards.

Guilds also provided education for the children of their members, again presumably taught by the village priest. At Finchingfield, Essex, the Guild of the Holy Trinity provided teaching for thirty scholars. After the suppression of the guilds in 1547, it was necessary, where a guild had endowed a grammar school, to submit a petition to retain the school. Whether these were generally granted is not clear and it seems that in the majority of cases schools were re-established through either public subscription or the commitment of a local benefactor. At Finchingfield a school was re-established for the poor children of the village and housed in the former guildhall. It seems that many former guildhalls were converted into schools, as the spacious first floor was ideal. Other buildings were also converted: at King's Norton, West Midlands, the former priest's house on the north side of the churchyard was used, and at Westbury on Severn, Gloucestershire, a chantry chapel in the churchyard. At Steeple Bumpstead, Essex, another small building became the village school in 1592; it is unlikely to have been built as a school for, like other public buildings of that date, it had an open ground floor. It was extensively altered in the eighteenth century and has been much restored since then. The church houses at Widecombe in the Moor and Cheriton Fitzpaine, both in Devon, and Chew Magna, Somerset, were all used as schools.

Not all early schools were housed in the church or in converted buildings, for from the sixteenth century purpose-built schools began to appear. Up until the Reformation the wealthy normally made endowments upon the church itself, which offered some hope for salvation in the afterlife. After this practice was abolished they often founded schools instead, and several survive from this period. One of the earliest forms part of the church complex at Ewelme, Oxfordshire. Founded by the Earl of Suffolk and his wife Alice in 1437, it has served the village for over five and a half centuries. Now a primary school, it is the oldest school still in its original building in the state system.

A grammar school was founded at Dedham, Essex, in 1574 by a wealthy cloth merchant and moved into the building in the Royal Square in 1732. It closed in 1889 and is now two houses. Behind the wooden shutters, on the soft red bricks, are the initials and dates of many of the past pupils. John Constable the painter was a pupil here.

In the seventeenth century the philanthropic impulse perhaps reached its height and many village schools were founded. The school at Uffington, in Oxfordshire, was founded in 1617 by Thomas Saunders of

Woolstone, who endowed 20 acres (8 ha) of land, the rent from which was 'towards the maynetenance and relieffe of the said Scholemaster for the teacheinge of twelve poor Schollars'. The endowed school was exclusively for boys; girls attended dame schools in the village. In 1851, a national school was built, with an infant school added in 1872, by which time Thomas Saunders's boys' school was in a dilapidated state and was closed. It is now a local museum.

125 *Old school, Uffington, Oxfordshire*

126 *John Brabin's School, Chipping, Lancashire*

Chipping, Lancashire, was at one time the centre of a thriving wool trade and John Brabin, a local dyer and wool merchant, was the village's most notable benefactor. He died in 1683 having the previous year, 'being infirme of body', drawn up a will leaving money for the relief of the poor and for the building of a village school. This school, in the centre of the village, served its original purpose from 1684 until new larger premises were built in 1880. John Brabin's School, which still benefits from his will, is still used by the community as a Sunday school and youth club.

Perhaps the most grandiose village school of this period is the one at Appleby Magna in Leicestershire, built by Sir John Moore at a cost of £2,339. Sir John, whose family had made a fortune in the East India trade, employed Sir Christopher Wren to design the building which housed two schools – the Grammar School and the English or Free School – each autonomous of the other. In 1904 they amalgamated to become the Boys' National School until 1933. The school is now the Sir John Moore Church of England (Aided) School.

The close connection between the church and education can be seen in the number of schools built in churchyards. The tiny seventeenth-century two-storeyed grammar school at Dent, Cumbria, is typical. It was originally founded to teach local boys to read and write and to master Church Latin and some mathematics. A few paces from the church at Constantine, Cornwall, is another. Built in 1733, it shows the extremely modest intentions of many of the early village schools.

The old grammar schools, which were established in some of the more prosperous villages, were places for the sons of the gentry and the more prosperous farmers and businessmen but not for the majority of village children. In 1818 only one in four children in England received any form of education and in early Victorian times the choice for the village children was between charity schools, dame schools, Sunday schools and schools of industry. They were all voluntary, but for the majority there was no school at all; any education they received was conducted in any available building – cottages, vicarages, church naves, barns and chapels. The school at Marshfield, Gloucestershire, was held in a room above the parish lock-up, at Minchinhampton, also in Gloucestershire, in the market hall and at Ampney Crucis, Gloucestershire, and Aynho, Northamptonshire, in a barn.

For most of the nineteenth century education remained voluntary,

127 *Former school house, Constantine, Cornwall*

with each community free to choose whether or not it would have a school and, if so, how it was to be run. Two major charitable societies developed: the National Society for the Education of the Poor in the Principles of the Established Church and the British System for the Education of the Labouring and Manufactory Classes of Society of Every Religious Persuasion. Their schools were known as 'National' and 'British' and both were voluntary societies receiving substantial grants from the government. However, some of the best charity schools to be founded in villages were endowed by local benefactors, voluntary donations or, in many cases, the 'school pence' in which each child contributed towards the teacher's salary. Even so, the enthusiasm for education was not universal; many squires only favoured minimal education to prevent their workforce having ideas above their station, while many farm labourers relied upon the money their children could earn from stone picking or bird scaring.

As early as 1833 state grants for school building were available through the churches, but it was not until the Act of 1870 that publicly controlled board schools, paid for out of local rates and governed by elected school boards, were established. In 1876 the principle was accepted that all children should receive elementary education, but not until 1880 was it compulsory for all children between the ages of five and ten, to attend school. In 1891 free education was made available to all children up to the age of fourteen.

Schools built during the Victorian and Edwardian periods are to be found in almost all our villages. Constructed of either stone or brick, often in a Gothic style, they have been at the heart of the village community for over a hundred years. Architecturally many of them are of little importance but a few are outstanding. Some resemble and are often mistaken for a church; Great Tew, in Oxfordshire, is one example, picturesquely situated on the village green.

Today, like so many other village institutions since the 1970s, the village school has been under threat. Many have now closed, the children being bused into larger, often new, schools in nearby villages as enrolment levels fall below the viable level. The village school is, perhaps, needed more now than ever, however, to preserve the community. Many of these redundant schools have been converted into dwellings, the smaller ones into single units, the larger ones into more than one. Others have been turned into community centres, village halls or youth clubs.

Inns, Public Houses and Alehouses

There can be few villages of any size that do not – or did not until recent times – possess a public house. In many cases it was for centuries one of the centres of village life, acting not only as a drinking house but also as a place where coroners held inquests, where magistrates met, where taxmen collected dues, where people held meetings, where villagers cast their vote in elections. In fact it was a real 'public house', a term first used in 1850.

Very few are, as sometimes claimed, medieval establishments. The majority are much later, although they may be housed in an older building. The Marlborough Head in Dedham, Essex, for example, dates from around 1430 and was built for a wealthy wool merchant, but, after the decline of the wool trade in the 1660s, the house was divided into an apothecary's

128 *The Marlborough Head, Dedham, Essex*

and a dyer's before the whole building became an inn in 1704. The frontage to the rear along Mill Lane, was originally the storage chamber. Likewise the Bull at Long Melford in Suffolk, built around 1450, also started life as the house of a wealthy cloth merchant before becoming an inn in around 1570. The White Hart at Fyfield, Oxfordshire, dates from the fifteenth century when Sir John Golafre, the lord of the manor, left enough money to build and endow a hospital or charity house for the poor to be run by a priest, who would pray for the soul of the founder. When this practice was outlawed by Henry VIII the hospital was sold to St John's College, Oxford, who have owned it ever since and leased it as a tavern. The original hall was divided into two floors. Many others started life as farmhouses; one such is the New Inn, Pembridge, Herefordshire, whose proximity to the village's market hall probably led to it becoming an alehouse, since the

129 *The New Inn, Pembridge, Herefordshire*

farmer would probably have brewed and sold ale at the local markets. Many others originated as cottages.

The story of some of our inns do nevertheless go back to medieval times. There were no inns as we know them today, but after the Norman Conquest every monastery founded a hospice in which travellers had the right to call at the gate and receive hospitality. These travellers were often pilgrims visiting one of the shrines at, for instance, Glastonbury, Chichester or Canterbury, or travelling merchants or soldiers. The Star Inn at Alfriston, East Sussex, is one of the finest examples of an old English hostelry. Founded in the thirteenth century by the Abbey of Battle as a hospice for pilgrims travelling to the shrine of St Richard at Chichester, parts of the present building date from around 1450 with a late fifteenth-century frontage. The Trout at Godstow, Oxfordshire, was originally a hospice attached to the local Benedictine nunnery, founded by Dame Ediva of Winchester. Ye Olde Bell at Hurley, Berkshire, was founded as a hospice attached to the Benedictine Priory of St Mary in 1135. At Norton St Philip, Somerset, the George Inn was built as a hospice by the Carthusian Priory of Hinton and also used as a storehouse for the local wool trade. The original stone building dates from 1397, but a fire destroyed the upper part, which was rebuilt in timber, probably in about 1500 or perhaps a little earlier.

Of course, where there was no hospice, taverns and alehouses had to provide for the needs of wayfarers. Alehouses have a long history in England and have been a feature since Saxon times, so much so that, in the tenth century, King Edgar limited the number to one in each village. However, because of the poor quality of drinking water, large quantities of ale were consumed, although it was much weaker than today. By the sixteenth century many villages supported two or three alehouses. They were often run by women, usually widows, who specialized in the brewing and selling of ale, many operating from ordinary farmhouses or cottages. The average alehouse was rather a seedy place, the drinks being served through what was known as a buttery bar, a Tudor innovation which was no more than a hatch through which the drinks were passed to the customers. These alehouses originally had to compete with church-ales brewed and sold by the church, but after 1571 these ceased. In Victorian times alehouses became even more numerous, most run by part-timers with a second trade, and it was not uncommon for villages to have several.

130 *The George Inn, Norton St Philip, Somerset*

Alehouses are today rare; many developed into public houses; the Horseshoes at Elsted, West Sussex, started life as an alehouse in Tudor times before expanding into the adjoining cottage. A few, however, have survived more or less unaltered; the Fleece at Bretforton, Worcestershire, was, like so many, a farmhouse until the 1840s and despite recent 'improvements' has survived in more or less its original state, giving some indication of what an alehouse was like. Originally there was no bar; a hatch served all three bars. Behind the hatch was the taproom, which also served as a beer cellar (as with many alehouses, there was no cellar). Again, as with most alehouses, the beer was brewed on the premises, stored in a shed at the rear, brought into the taproom and served from the hatch. The hatch has recently been enlarged and hand pumps fitted. The building is now owned by the National Trust.

131 *The Fleece, Bretforton, Worcestershire*

Another alehouse which has retained its old character is the King's Head at Laxfield, Suffolk. Known locally as the Low House, it was originally one of three inns in the village – The General Wolfe, at the top, was known as the Top House, the Royal Oak, in the centre, as the Middle House and the King's Head, at the other end, by the stream, as the Low House. Now only the King's Head remains as an inn, with the beer still served from a cask in a back room, the central room still being the settle room, with its splendid high-backed, wooden settles around the walls, and smaller rooms around, with bare boards and Victorian furniture. The Mounted Rifleman in the hamlet of Elverton, on the edge of Luddenham Marshes, Kent, has also remained almost unaltered over the centuries: there are two rooms, but no bar as such. The smaller bar has a serving area with a hatch, and the drinks are brought up from the cellar for the customers. An inscription above the door 'Tomson & Wotton 1634 Old Brewery' perhaps gives an indication of its age.

Taverns, like alehouses, go back centuries and, in addition to being drinking houses also provided accommodation, although this was often poor. By 1590 the hospices had gone and an increasing number of taverns began to appear to receive travellers.

Wealthy travellers would seek out the manor house for hospitality. In some cases, the lord of the manor would vacate his manor house for a larger home, turning it into an inn or even, in some instances, specially

132 *The King's Head, Laxfield, Suffolk*

erecting a guesthouse to be run as an inn by his steward. The Grantley Arms, Wonersh, Surrey, is a typical example, having been built in the fifteenth century as a manor house.

The Elizabethans were great travellers and, to accommodate the increasing number of travellers, many new inns were built and others enlarged, dispensing food and lodgings as well as ale. By the beginning of the seventeenth century the English inn was already well established. A great European traveller of this period Fynes Moryson, tells us in his *Itinerary* of 1617 that 'the world affords no such inns of England both either for pleasure or cheap entertainment'. Nevertheless there must have been many villages that were still poorly served.

It was the eighteenth century that was the great period for inn-building and particularly for the conversion, improvement and enlargement of existing inns, including the building of stable blocks and better accommodation. Following the Turnpike Act of 1663, roads slowly began to improve and by the late eighteenth century there were over 20,000 miles of turnpike roads, all crowded with traffic – coaches, post-chaises and horse riders. In 1784, John Palmer of Bath introduced his revolutionary plan to carry mail by coach and posting houses sprang up along the main routes, with the innkeeper acting as local postmaster. Early in the nineteenth century Thomas Telford and John Macadam produced still better road surfaces and by 1835 most main roads had been macadamized. Evidence of the coaching inns and posting houses which sprang up along these routes, where horses could be changed, can be seen in many of our villages. The characteristic features are the large opening to the front, which admitted the coach and horses to the yard and extensive stabling for the horses at the rear. Many old timber-framed inns were given pretentious Georgian fronts at this time, and these inns often became important social centres, attracting nobility and gentry.

The years between 1800 and 1835 were the golden age for these inns, but the coming of the railways in the 1830s began to hit the coaching trade and consequently the coaching inns. By 1845 most long-distance passenger traffic had been captured by the railways and many of the coaching inns were sold; some became houses and others declined in importance to become just local public houses. Standards in general began to decline and competition was often fierce between many poorly furnished inns and alehouses. In Victorian times it was not uncommon for larger villages to have ten or more inns, public houses and alehouses.

Corfe Castle in Dorset had twelve such establishments. In 1869 the Wine and Beerhouse Act gave local justices control over premises where alcohol could be consumed, and this saw the end of many of the seedier establishments. With the rapid advancement of the brewing industry many were forced to give up or become tied to a brewery.

At the end of the nineteenth century the village inns and alehouses served a declining population, but at the beginning of the twentieth century new mechanical methods of transport brought about a revival in their fortunes. At first many began to cater for the touring cyclists and by 1937 the Cyclists Touring Club had some 4,000 inns on its books, each having the club sign and providing bed and breakfast. Then in the 1930s the increasing popularity of the motor car made their revival certain. However, in the last century the number of licensed houses has dropped by over a third and is continuing to decline especially in those villages that are some distance from the local town and have to rely on locals.

Shops

There seems little doubt that the early 'shops' in England were no more than stalls or booths set up in the market places or at fairs. The weekly markets provided all that was necessary for the village, while the annual fairs, with their temporary booths, provided additional goods not produced locally.

Although there are a few small shops, mainly dating from the thirteenth century, in some of our medieval towns, in the villages the earliest surviving examples are of timber construction, for as we have seen our stone village buildings are rarely earlier than sixteenth-century. Timber-framed shop fronts dating from the fifteenth and sixteenth centuries have survived here and there. From an examination of these medieval structures it is evident that the shop front comprised two or three unglazed openings, generally with a four-centred arch set below a square head. They often have some form of rebate to take an internal shutter or else the unglazed windows were secured at night by a pair of timber shutters, the upper one hinged from above, the lower one from below. Both shutters opened outwards, the lower one let down to serve as an external counter during the day and the upper one raised to provide shelter for the counter. These shutters can still be seen on a surviving medieval shop at Lavenham, Suffolk, preserved beneath a later covering of plaster and only in recent years revealed. In most cases where these medieval shop fronts survive they have been filled in with plaster or glazed, as in the house in Abbey Street, Cerne Abbas, in Dorset. In some instances the unglazed opening was filled with a timber lattice, as can be seen at the medieval shop front at Charing, Kent.

133 *Tudor shop front, Cerne Abbas, Dorset*

Not all early shop fronts were divided into two or three openings; many had a single, larger opening, again with shutters, a type that survived well into the eighteenth century. These unglazed fronts continue to be used for some trades even today, particularly for butchers and greengrocers. One example is the butcher's shop at Brenchley, Kent, a sixteenth-century timber-framed building. At Hambledon, Hampshire, there is a building that is no longer used as a shop but retains its old shutters, forming a counter protected by a small hipped roof.

It was not until the late sixteenth century that village shops began to be recorded. Probate records clearly show an increased number of tradesmen with retail businesses and, although most were in market towns, a few became established in some of the larger villages. During the seventeenth century the number of retailers gradually increased until, by the 1680s, they had set up even in some of the smaller villages. The distinction between manufacture, wholesale trade and retail selling was often unclear, for many craftsmen would sell both wholesale and retail as appropriate. In many cases craftsmen and specialists also sold other articles not related to their trade, tending towards general retailing. For instance drapers (dealers in woollen and linen) and mercers (dealers in silk) often stocked groceries as well as tobacco, medicine and even items of ironmongery. However, many of the items stocked in the seventeenth and eighteenth centuries appear to be luxury goods well out of the reach of ordinary villagers, who had to rely on the many assorted hawkers who formed an important part of everyday village life.

By the first quarter of the nineteenth century few villages were without retail outlets and the number increased throughout that century. Soon most villages had several shops – general stores where one could buy almost everything and a few specialists retailers like a butcher, a baker, a bootmaker and perhaps a chemist and druggist, a tailor or a draper.

With the spread of the railways a wide range of mass-produced items began to arrive in the villages. Imported goods that were once luxuries, like tea, coffee and sugar, began to fall in price and most villagers could now afford them and wanted to buy them regularly. Village shops began to stock them, together with other affordable household goods, like factory-made biscuits, chocolates, cutlery, soap, cottons and cheap china. The demand for these and other products increased and the number of village shops continued to grow, reaching their peak in the 1880s.

Many of the shopkeepers were merely part-time traders who kept a shop as a sideline, or were spinsters or widows who eked out a living conducting their business from the front room of their cottage or farmhouse, using an existing window to display their goods. As business developed windows were often enlarged, shop fronts were inserted and internal partitions were removed to make the village stores which are still seen. Very few purpose-built shops were constructed in villages.

Diversity remained vital and many shopkeepers were hard to classify. When contracts were first offered in the 1840s to run post offices they were an important adjunct to the village shops' business.

However, the combination of shop and post office was not as usual in the mid-nineteenth century as it became later, and only about half the village post offices were linked with shops. It was these that were best placed to survive when, in the early 1920s, the village shop first felt the decline in trading that increased mobility brought.

Today modern transport and the evolution since the 1950s of the village, from a self-contained, locally employed community into a largely residential one, has inevitably taken its toll. Shopkeepers, like other independent traders, face continuing competition from the supermarkets and chain stores now that most people have easy access to nearby towns. Only in larger villages, which often serve surrounding smaller villages, those that are remote or those that are in areas of tourism do village stores have a chance to survive.

134 *The Old Post Office, Cropthorne, Worcestershire*

135 The Post Office, Mansell Lacey, Herefordshire

SIX

Agricultural and Industrial Buildings

Until the twentieth century agriculture was the mainstay of rural England. Before the introduction of enclosures, farms were located within the village, and it was not until the land was enclosed that farmers began to build their new houses away from the village, on their newly acquired lands. Former farmhouses are to be found in a great many villages, and in those where enclosures were late to arrive farmsteads continued to be built in the villages and still survive.

England did not become a fully industrialized nation until the nineteenth century. As we have seen, before the development of water and steam power to drive machinery and such inventions as Arkwright's water-frame and Crompton's mule in the 1770s, industry was largely carried on in people's own houses or in small workshops, and was widely distributed over the countryside, rather than being concentrated in large industrial towns. Along the coast fishing was important.

In eastern England, amongst the agriculture-related industries, malting, brewing and milling have left the most remains; in Bedfordshire straw-plaiting, straw-hatting, and lace-making flourished; in the south-eastern counties, East Anglia, parts of the Pennines, the Cotswolds and elsewhere, weaving and its associated trades were, for many centuries, thriving industries; Leicestershire and Nottinghamshire were centres of framework knitting, while in Northamptonshire and the southern part of Leicestershire there was the boot and shoe industry. In addition there were coopers, carpenters, blacksmiths, wheelwrights, tanners and builders, and their often humble yards and workshops still add scale and dignity to many villages.

Away from the villages there were the extractive industries; tin mining in Devon and Cornwall, lead mining in Derbyshire, on Dartmoor and elsewhere, quarrying in many parts of the country as well as brickmaking, and all have left their mark on the landscape if not the village. The ruins of old tin and lead mines provide evocative, even romantic features to many isolated areas of the country.

Today many of these agricultural and industrial buildings have become redundant, often demolished, left derelict or put to other uses. Old farm buildings no longer meet the needs of modern agriculture and barns and other large buildings have often been converted into dwellings, as have many watermills and the occasional windmill. Others have been adapted for use by light industry and crafts. Sadly many other rural buildings, which were often rough and simple structures, have disappeared.

Workshops

Today villages are generally quiet and empty, but before the coming of the car they were busy, bustling places. Although many villagers would have been working away from the village, in the fields or on the estate, others worked within the village, making and supplying many of the necessities of life. Workshops of various types, therefore, formed an important part of the village scene. All villages depended heavily on their blacksmiths, wheelwrights, carpenters and builders, while the larger ones also supported cobblers, coopers, shoemakers, thatchers, stonemasons and perhaps tailors and dressmakers. Although some of these were undertaken at home, others required workshops.

In many villages the blacksmith was regarded as the most important craftsman and few would not have had at least one. Indeed in the heyday of the horse, many would have more. Dedham in Essex at one time supported no less than eight. Closely associated with the blacksmith was the farrier, the two crafts often being undertaken by the same person, but after about 1890 farriery as a separate craft seems to have disappeared. The coming of factory-made tools and the demise of the farm horse also put most village smithies out of business. Some have continued up to the present, shoeing the occasional horse, repairing farm machinery and making wrought iron but there are probably fewer than 1,000 smithies today compared with some 112,000 in 1891.

Smithies like many buildings used for crafts, were often rough and simple structures, using materials which came easily to hand, and once they ceased to trade, they soon became derelict. Many have disappeared or been put to other uses, like the one at Penshurst, Kent, which now forms part of the village garage, and the famous one at Godmanstone, Dorset, which is now a pub, claiming to be the smallest in England. It was granted a license to sell ale by Charles II, who stopped there to have his horse shod.

Many forges still survive, although they are not always still used. They were built of local material in the local tradition, but as with so many craft buildings, no universal design was adopted. They were often built adjoining

136 *Forge, Claverdon, Warwickshire*

137 *Village smithy, Ford, Northumberland*

the craftsmen's houses and in some cases have either been incorporated in the house or are used as an outbuilding. Some are distinguished by the doorway being framed in the shape of a horseshoe, like the one on the green at Ickwell Green, Bedfordshire, and those at Claverdon, Warwickshire and at Ford, Northumberland.

Closely associated with the blacksmith was the wheelwright, who often used the former's facilities to heat the iron rims for the wheels. Unlike the blacksmith, who was a master of iron, the wheelwright worked not only with iron but also with wood, for he not only produced wheels but complete carts and wagons, which incorporated local designs and regional preferences. Because carts and wagons lasted up to fifty years, there was often insufficient custom for the wheelwright to concentrate solely on his main craft and many turned to allied trades, becoming carpenters as well as undertakers, making coffins. The Josselyn family of Belstead in Suffolk traded as wheelwrights and coffin-makers in the village until modern times. Generally wheelwrights' workshops are of similar construction to the smithy but are smaller, and few now remain. At Dedham, Essex, a timber-framed building, once a wheelwright's shop, has been converted into a garage. At East Walton in Norfolk there is an unusual survivor: a small wheelwright's oven, which was used to

138 *Wheelwright's oven, East Walton, Norfolk*

heat the iron rims prior to fixing them to the wheels. The building dates from around 1850 and was last used in about 1940. It was restored in 1977, with further repairs carried out in 1990.

Although most industries were carried out at home, many required looms and space to set them up and so this part of the work was sometimes done in the master clothiers' house. There is a fine example of a timber-framed clothier's hall at Biddenham in Kent, which was obviously occupied by clothworkers; workshops were built during the sixteenth century and enlarged several times, with the east gable, dated 1672, being the final addition. Another can be found at Dedham, Essex. A fine timber-framed structure built at the beginning of the fifteenth century, it comprised living quarters, a workroom, offices and a warehouse around a courtyard. The layout is now not clear but the

139 *Southfields, Dedham, Essex*

south-west wing was called the master weaver's house, while the upper floor of the east wing was one long room. The last clothier was Henry Sida, who went bankrupt for the sum of £1,500 in 1747. Around 1800 the building was converted into ten tenements by the addition of brick and slate lean-tos and the insertion of chimney stacks.

For 200 years the cloth industry brought great prosperity to south-eastern and eastern England, but by the latter part of the seventeenth century it had declined, and died out in the eighteenth century. At Goudhurst, Kent, however, even in 1725 when the industry was in decline, there were over twenty looms, each employing eighteen women and several men.

Up until the nineteenth century most weaving and framework knitting was carried out in the home on hand looms, but, with the introduction of wider frames, it became necessary to construct workshops separate from the weavers' cottages to house them. In Nottinghamshire and Leicestershire, the centres for framework knitting, frameworkers constructed buildings, normally of two storeys, with rows of windows along each side and the frames crammed tightly along the walls leaving a narrow gangway between. A few still survive: at Chapel Street, Ruddington, Nottinghamshire, there is one built in 1829, with the workshops to the rear of the property containing the knitting machines on two floors, as well as coal sheds, stores, bucket closets and a pigsty. To the front of the property was a block of four houses consisting of two 'through' houses at each end with two rooms on each floor, and two back-to-back houses in the centre with one room on each floor. The water for the whole complex was supplied from a pump in the central yard. The property is now a museum run by the Ruddington Framework Knitters' Shops Preservation Trust.

In Leicestershire, by the early nineteenth century, small framework shops, either separate from or built onto a house, began to appear to house the wide frames which were producing cut-and-sew knitted fabric rather than fully fashioned stockings. At the village of Shepshed the development of the hosiery industry can be followed in several buildings, from a timber-framed cottage with two knitters' windows in an extension, to a single-storeyed workshop and a master hosier's house with frameshop and finishing rooms attached. Soon larger workshops were provided to house groups of these frames: good examples can be seen at Ratby where two large workshops, built around 1860, stand in a brick-paved yard, each two-storeyed with long rows of windows at the ends as well as the sides. In northern Northamptonshire and southern Leicestershire similar work-

140 *Thorne House, Low Hartsop, Cumbria*

shops were built for the boot and shoe industry, and when the hosiery industry in Leicestershire was finally mechanized some of those workshops were adopted for this use, for the boot and shoe industry remained a hand craft for much longer.

A local characteristic, once common in the Lake District, was the so-called spinning gallery. Forming part of a house, barn or other outbuilding, it was not used for spinning, despite its name, but for drying wool. These galleries first appeared in the sixteenth century and were so common in the nineteenth that they were considered the most striking architectural peculiarity in the Lake District. Today these galleries are rare but can still be found; Thorne House, Low Hartsop, and one at Townend, Troutbeck, both in Cumbria, are notable examples.

In the Midlands the chain-, nail- and file-makers often had forge hearths, built in their gardens. Few now remain *in situ* but there is one at Belper in Derbyshire, which up until the 1770s, when cotton mills were introduced, was a small village specializing in the production of nails. At the Avoncroft Museum of Buildings at Stoke Prior in Worcestershire another, which came originally from nearby Bromsgrove, has been re-erected. Also at the museum is a chain-making workshop, formerly located at Cradley in the West Midlands, which is typical of many which once existed. Redditch in Worcestershire was the centre of the needle-making industry and Forge Mill was converted to a scouring mill, used to clean the finished needles. It is the oldest surviving scouring mill in the world, and is now the home of the National Needle Museum. Work was also carried out in the surrounding villages; at Feckenham there still stands a small needle-making factory (now converted into a house).

Coastal villages had trades and industries associated with the sea and fishing but today little remains of them, for many villages' fishing was fated to collapse in the face of competition from larger ports, with their large deep-sea fishing boats, larger markets and, with the coming of the railways, nationwide distribution of the catch. Few buildings remain related to fishing, but at Tollesbury in Essex there are still the old timber-framed, weatherboarded fishermen's lofts, now restored and put to other uses.

Warehouses

Warehouses are not normally associated with villages, but some coastal villages and inland ports built them, and some still survive, although most have been converted to other uses. Many coastal villages flourished as trading ports, with harbours capable of handling small craft. Along the northern Norfolk coast there are several villages which were at one time bustling ports. The waterfront at Blakeney was a commercial port until the beginning of the last century. The estuary has now silted up and only small pleasure craft can sail up the narrow channel but the quay still has several buildings that reflect its former importance. Another former port is Cley next the Sea, now over a mile inland but once second only to King's Lynn in Norfolk in importance. In medieval times it was centred around the church but in the seventeenth century reclamation work finally forced new wharfs to be erected near deep water. With the destruction by fire of the old town, new buildings were built around the wharfs. Today traces of the old quay remains, dominated by an early eighteenth-century windmill.

With the coming of the canals inland ports began to be developed; Shardlow in Derbyshire was one of the most important, first providing wharfs to handle coal and timber and, in the 1770s, red-brick warehouses for such varied goods as iron, cheese, salt from Shropshire and locally grown corn to be shipped to the industrial cities. It also had thriving port industries, including rope-making, sail-making, crane and boatbuilding. It prospered until the coming of the railway, when business began to decline and it slowly sank into obscurity. Its most imposing building is the Clock Warehouse which stands, with its distinctive clock, near the bridge where the busy London road crosses the canal. Built in 1780 this fine red brick and tile building has been restored and now houses a restaurant and canal museum. Further into Shardlow are other former warehouses, the low Iron Warehouse and the Malt Warehouse, with flattened over-hanging corners to avoid damage from wagons, being two of the finest. There were many other canalside developments, for instance at Stoke Bruerne on the Grand Union Canal in Northamptonshire, which supported small warehouses. One is now a canal museum.

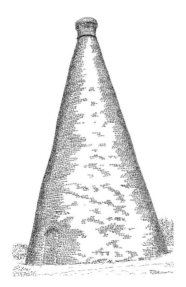

141 *Brick kiln, Nettlebed, Oxfordshire*

Kilns

❧

Early brick-making was a highly localized trade, the bricks being made from local earth, often dug close to the site of the new building. During the seventeenth century, as bricks became popular, small brickworks sprang up through south-east and eastern England and the Midlands. Today few remain, but reminders of their former presence are to be found on occa-sions. One such place is Nettlebed in Oxfordshire, where brick-making can be traced back to the sixteenth century.

There were several kilns here but only one survives. It dates from the eighteenth century and was last used in 1927.

Watermills

Water was almost certainly the earliest form of power to be harnessed for human needs. The Domesday survey records that between 1080 and 1086 there were 5,268 watermills. Although many existing mills were built on the sites of Domesday ones, none of them can be dated further back than the sixteenth century. Moreover the majority would have passed through a number of complete or partial rebuilds. Machinery in particular needed regular replacement and little survives from earlier than the eighteenth century.

Watermills, both large and small, are still a feature of the country-side throughout England, the fast-flowing rivers and streams of the highland areas providing more power than the gentle, slow-flowing rivers to be found over much of the lowland zone. In the east, the south and the south-east most are timber-framed and clad with weather-boarding; elsewhere they are usually of brick or stone.

Two forms were built: one beside the mill stream with the wheel to one side, the other bridging the stream, with the wheel inside the building. Watermills can also be identified by the position at which the water strikes the wheel; an undershot wheel is turned by water flowing through the vanes at the bottom first, with an overshot wheel it strikes the top first. An overshot wheel, usually placed on a man-made or natural weir, is the more efficient of the two, needing only a quarter of the volume of water to provide the same amount of power.

Not all watermills used rivers to drive the wheels. In some coastal areas, particularly in Essex and Suffolk and parts of the south, the ebb and flow of the tides provided the motive power. Tide-mills, as these mills were called, were usually located along shallow creeks, often miles from the coast, where a pound was constructed to hold the water of the incoming tide. Today there are few capable of working. There are two in eastern England, one at Woodbridge in Suffolk and the other at Thorrington in Essex. The one at Thorrington is at the head of a creek leading off the Colne estuary between Wivenhoe and Brightlingsea. The present building dates from 1831, but mills have been sited here from at least the beginning of the seventeenth century. The wheel failed in 1926 and a portable steam engine was brought in to provide power for the three pairs of stones. The last private owner was Tom Glover, who retired and maintained both the mill and its pound until in 1974 it was purchased by Essex County Council and restored to working order. Another tide-mill which is still working is at Eling in Hampshire. The present Georgian brick-built building, built on the site of a much older mill, was abandoned in the 1940s and restored to full working order in the 1980s.

142 Tide-mill, Thorrington, Essex

The principal use of watermills was grinding corn but water power was also used in various other industries. From the middle of the sixteenth century, the iron industry depended on it to turn its machinery. The machinery in hammer-mills operated huge tilt-hammers which were used to refine the iron by reheating it and beating it. The bellows for the furnace could also be operated in this way, the water being provided by reserves in vast hammer-ponds, which were formed by damming rivers.

The Weald of Kent and Sussex was, at the end of the sixteenth century, an important iron-producing centre, for it could provide the raw material: iron ore in the form of ironstone, fuel in the form of timber, and water power. At the end of Elizabeth's reign ironworks existed in Kent and by the early part of the seventeenth century in Sussex. Here and there in the Weald, ponds are still found, whose names indicate their former use: Furnace Pond or Hammer Pond.

The mill at Burton in West Sussex was being used as an iron forge in 1635, with water-powered trip-hammers producing wrought-iron weapons and tools. Warnham Mill, also in West Sussex, was used to smelt ironstone dug locally, with the two wheels driving the bellows for the double furnace. The mill was destroyed by the Roundheads in the Civil War in 1645, rebuilt as a corn mill and operated until 1928. By the end of the seventeenth century the Wealden iron industry had ceased, losing out to other parts of the country where better ore and coal were to be found.

The other principal use of water power was in the textile industry. Up until the beginning of the eighteenth century most of the weaving of woollens, cottons and lace was carried out on hand-looms, but with the coming of James Hargreaves's spinning jenny, it began to be switched to factories using water power. There was still a problem producing strong enough thread or wrap yarn but this was overcome first by Sir Richard Arkwright's water-frame spinning machine which, unlike the spinning jenny, did not require highly skilled operators, and then by Samuel Crompton's spinning mule, which enabled a very fine wrap yarn to be produced. The preferred power for spinning machines was water, supplied by a fast-flowing stream, and in 1771 Richard Arkwright built the first water-powered cotton-spinning mill in England at Cromford in Derbyshire. In the Pennines, too, water was readily available, but Watt's steam engine offered a more reliable source of power, which was eventually adopted, firstly for spinning and

143 *Fulling mill, New Alresford, Hampshire*

carding and then gradually for weaving, which proved rather more resistant to change.

Many of the early water mills concentrated on carding the raw wool in order to prepare it for spinning. In the Pennines many, like Shore Mill, Delph, Lancashire, date from the latter part of the eighteenth century. Built during the early 1780s, it is a three-storeyed stone building with mullioned windows, a characteristic of a local weaver's dwelling, and still retains the local vernacular style of architecture in its external appearance. Fulling, the process of cleaning and treating the wool cloth, was another process done by water power, compressing the fabric with fulling stocks comprising wedge-shaped hammers. Before the introduction of this system the cloth was put into troughs with water and fuller's earth and trodden on.

Water mills were also used for other industrial purposes: the grinding of flint for use in the manufacture of pottery (Cheddleton Flint Mill), gypsum-grinding, paper-making and needle-making, for example. These mills were often converted from corn-grinding, and in some instances the wheels provided power for two separate operations; the one at Dursley, Gloucestershire, for example powered both a pair of grinding stones and a pair of fulling stocks. During the nineteenth century many of these industrial mills, as well as some used for corn, were converted to steam power.

Like so many other old industrial buildings few watermills are still

144 *Shalford Mill, Surrey*

145 *Lode Mill, Cambridgeshire*

in working order. Some, however, are operated by the Traditional Cornmillers' Guild, which was set up in 1987 by a group of independent millers to use natural power to produce stoneground meals and flours. Charlecote Mill, Hampton Lucy, Warwickshire, and Headley Mill, Bordon, Hampshire, still produce wholewheat flour and animal feed.

Many have been bought and restored, either by local authorities or local preservation societies. Pakenham Mill in Suffolk, which ceased to operate in 1974, was restored by the Suffolk Preservation

146 *Nether Alderley Mill, Cheshire*

147 *Corpusty Mill, Norfolk*

Society between 1978 and 1981 and Woods Mill, Henfield, in West Sussex, has been preserved by and is headquarters of the Sussex Trust for Nature. The National Trust owns several, including Shalford Mill in Surrey, an early eighteenth-century example presented to the Trust in 1932, Lode Mill in Cambridgeshire, which forms part of the Anglesey Abbey Estate, Houghton Mill, also in Cambridgeshire and Nether Alderley Mill, Alderley Edge, Cheshire, which was built in 1581 and presented to the Trust in 1950. Many have been converted to other uses: some have become private houses, such as Corpusty Mill in Norfolk or flats, as at Hambleden Mill, Buckinghamshire; others have been converted into restaurants. Some are being used for other trades; the mill at Lower Slaughter in Gloucestershire, for example, is now a bakery.

148 *Lower Slaughter Mill, Gloucestershire*

Windmills

~

Unlike watermills, no windmills were recorded in the Domesday Book. The first reference dates from 1185, when a windmill in the village of Weedley, Yorkshire, was let at a rent of 8s per year, while the first illustration of one appeared in the *English Windmill Psalter*, which is believed to have been written around 1260. From the thirteenth century they spread throughout England until at one time as many as 10,000 were at work. They were more numerous in the fairly flat, corn-growing lowland counties of Kent, Sussex, Surrey, Essex, Suffolk, Cambridgeshire, Norfolk, Lincolnshire and the East Midlands, where there was a lack of water power. In the highland zone, where there are many streams, there were few windmills, although Somerset had a reasonable number.

At the end of the nineteenth century the corn mill began to decline, just when its design was at its peak. The reason for this was mainly the construction of steam mills at the large ports, which ground large quantities of foreign grain. The decline was accelerated during and after the First World War when, owing to government regulations, many millers were forced to grind only animal feed.

The earliest windmills in this country were post-mills; the name comes from the great post known as the main post on which the body, which contained the machinery, turned to face the wind. Supporting the main post were four raking quarterbars, each morticed into the main post at one end with the other framed to crosstrees. The main post was quartered over the crosstrees but not supported by them. The crosstrees were originally laid directly on or buried beneath the surface of the ground to give the mill greater stability but later they were raised on brick piers. The top of the main post either had a pintle, turned out of the solid, or an iron gudgeon or Sampson head – a cap and bearing of iron. Pivoting and rotating on top of this was a great transverse beam, called the crowntree, around which the timber body of the mill was constructed.

Early post-mills had simple pitched roofs, like the one at Bourn, Cambridgeshire, but later curved rafters were generally used to accommodate a larger brake wheel. At Cromer Mill in Hertfordshire an ogee roof can be seen, the rafters being shaped to follow a reverse curve to a point at the ridge. The body of the mill was generally covered with weatherboarding painted white or tarred. Access to the mill body was by means of a wide ladder from the ground up to the platform at the rear of the lower floor. Many mills had a canopy over the door; which varied greatly from mill to mill. The early post-mills were of the open-trestle type, but in the late eighteenth century roundhouses began to be added to give protection to the substructure and to provide extra storage space. These roundhouses were not attached to the mill in any

149 *Post-mill, Pitstone, Buckinghamshire*

150 *Post-mill, Dale Abbey, Derbyshire*

way, the main-post passing through an opening at the apex of the roof. Later, many mills in eastern Suffolk had the roundhouse built at the same time as the mill itself; some had as many as three floors and were as tall as the body of the mill proper. Mills were sometimes raised when the roundhouse was constructed; the mill at Saxtead Green was raised a total of three times, the last probably in 1854.

The logical development of the post-mill was the tower-mill, with a fixed tower built of brick or stone and a timber cap, which was the only part to be turned to face the wind. Early tower-mills were short, with conical caps, and cylindrical so that the sails could clear the face. The early ones were usually of two or three floors, which enabled the common sails to be set by hand from the ground. The cap was turned into the wind by means of a tail pole. Later, the towers were built with a batter giving them greater stability and allowing more room at the base, where space was needed. This was done by having the windshaft inclined rather than horizontal, as in the early mills. Most tower-mills had five or six floors with a stage at the first or second, from which the miller could adjust the sails. The caps of these tower-mills were their most distinguishing feature, and were considered their crowning glory. They varied greatly, not only in size but also in shape. Basically there were five types: gabled, boat-shaped, wagonshaped, domed and ogee.

151 *Tower-mill, Billingford, Norfolk*

A variation of the tower-mill is the smock-mill, which derived its name from its likeness to the linen smock, once the traditional dress of the English countryman. It was a tapering timber tower covered with weatherboarding. Generally they were octagonal in shape but there were also six-, ten- and twelve-sided ones constructed. Most were built on a brick base, which was sometimes only a few courses high, as at Stelling Minnis in Kent, but generally comprised one, two or even three floors. Smock-mills are generally found in Kent, Sussex and the southern part of Essex, although the oldest surviving one is at Lacey Green in Buckinghamshire, which is reported to have been built in 1650 and moved from Chesham to its present site in 1821.

The early sails were lattice-like frameworks covered with canvas. The sail area was on the driving side, with a narrow board, inclined at an angle, attached to that side to assist the flow of wind to the canvas. Known as common sails, they had one great disadvantage: when the wind strength changed, the area of sail could not be changed without first stopping the mill and bringing each sail to its lowest position in turn. In 1772 Andrew Meikle, a Scottish millwright, introduced the spring sail, which was designed to 'spill the wind' during squalls and storms. The canvas was replaced with a number of small, rectangular, hinged shutters which opened as the wind increased. It was less powerful than the common sail and it was not unusual to use two common sails in conjunction with two spring sails. In 1789 Captain Stephen Hooper invented the roller reefing sail, replacing the shutters with roller blinds, but the most important development occurred in about 1807 when Sir William Cubitt devised his patent sail. For this he combined the shutters of the spring sail with the control of the roller reefer sail, so that for the first time they could 'spill the wind' without the need to stop the mill. Most mills had four sails but some sixty or seventy had five, six or eight. These are today found mainly in Lincolnshire.

It was essential that the sails of a mill remained at all times square into the eye of the wind, for it was designed and balanced to resist pressure from the front, not the rear. It was, therefore, necessary to be able to turn it into the wind, a process known as luffing or winding the mill. The simplest form of winding gear was the tail pole, a large pole to the rear of the mill, with which the miller turned the mill manually. Tail-poles were generally used on post-mills, but early smaller tower- and smock-mills also used this device. As smock- and tower-mills increased in height it became necessary to improve the way the cap was turned. In 1745 a fully automatic method of winding the mill was patented by Edmund Lee. This was a small wind wheel comprising between five and ten vanes covered with boarding and set at right angles to the sails. It was mounted, in the case of post-mills, either to the tail-pole or to the steps, and in the case of tower- and smock-mills, to the cap. While the sails remained square into the wind this fantail remained stationary, being sheltered by the body of the mill, but as soon as the wind changed direction it struck the side of the vanes and set it in motion, turning the mill until the sails once again faced into the wind.

Although the majority of mills were used for grinding corn or other cereals, many, like watermills, were used for other purposes. Snuff, mustard and, vegetable oils were all ground, but by far the greatest use apart from corn-milling was in the drainage of land, particularly in the Norfolk Broads and the Fens. These drainage-mills, like corn-mills, were superseded first by steam and later by oil and electric pumps, and although some were built on the Broads as late as 1914, their decline was rapid and by the 1950s all had stopped operating. Today many are derelict but, over the last forty years or so, some have been restored; those at Stracey Arms, Horsey Mere and Berney Arms are notable examples.

152 *Drainage-mill, Berney Arms, Norfolk*

153 *Tower-mill, Cley next the Sea, Norfolk*

Like watermills, some windmills have been converted into dwellings and those at Cley next the Sea, Burnham Overy and Weybourne, all in Norfolk, Great Bardfield in Essex and Morcott in Rutland are all fine examples. These remain true to the outward appearance of the original mills, but unfortunately others have been converted less sympathetically. Like other former industrial and agriculture buildings a very special approach is required if the character of the building is to be retained.

Maltings

Malting is the process of preparing barley for brewing by steeping, germinating and kiln-drying it. Its origins are obscure but it was an essential household activity, continuing on a domestic scale from the Middle Ages to the end of the eighteenth century. Even in the sixteenth century, however, professional maltsters provided malt to the growing brewery trade, as well as to household brewers. Although early malthouses were small structures, in the late nineteenth century, particularly in the arable regions of eastern England, the industry developed rapidly, mainly in response to the repeal of the malt tax in 1880, and maltings became larger and increasingly industrialized. Large brick structures began to appear, not only in major local ports such as Ipswich and King's Lynn (reflecting the preference for coastal locations which received cheap grain imports from North America), but also in villages such as Long Melford and Stratford St Mary, both in Suffolk. At Mistley, on the River Stour in Essex, the village developed around seven large maltings.

Because of the nature of these highly specialized buildings they are now redundant. Like many other rural buildings, they have often been converted into houses or flats, or are simply used as storage. Many of the small village maltings associated with home brewing and local alehouses have disappeared; a few have been converted into attractive houses, such as the one at Foxton in Cambridgeshire, which was converted in 1870.

Barns

~

Like so many other aspects of traditional life in England, farm buildings fall into two contrasting zones; the highland zone to the north and west, which was largely pastoral, and the lowland zone to the south and east, which was largely arable. The arable farms needed at least one important building, the barn, which tended to dominate the farmstead. With pastoral farming, on the other hand, the barns were small, reflecting the lesser importance of the corn crop. The word 'barn' comes from the old English *bern*, which meant 'barley house', barley being the main crop of the Anglo-Saxon farmers.

The most impressive barns are therefore to be found in the lowland zone, for it was the most important working building, dominating many homesteads from the Middle Ages to Hanoverian times. Its main functions were to provide safe storage for the unthreshed corn crop, to give shelter to the threshers working through the winter, and to store the threshed straw before its use as litter and fodder for the cattle. The threshing floor, on which the threshers flailed the corn, lay across the barn between doors, which were large enough for a full laden wagon to pass through. The threshing floor was constructed of flagstones, timber or beaten earth, and had to be hard enough to withstand the beating of the flails. Large barns often had two threshing floors and two sets of doors.

The oldest surviving barns are the medieval monastic granges, the earliest dating from the late twelfth or early thirteenth century, but these were more like huge warehouses than working farm buildings. Some impressive medieval tithe barns still exist. The early fourteenth-century one at Great Coxwell, in Oxfordshire, which once belonged to the Cistercian abbey of Beaulieu, is some 152 feet (46.3 metres) long and stands in a cluster of farm buildings along a narrow lane leading to the village church. Both the buttressed walls and the stone tiles covering the massive roof, which more than doubles the height of the building, are of Cotswold stone. Even larger is the one at Middle Littleton, Worcestershire, which was built of coursed Lias and is some 316 feet (96.3 metres) long and buttressed like a church. It was built by the Benedictine monks of Evesham Abbey and dates from about 1315. It has an aisled bay at either end with eight base-cruck trusses

154 *Ashleworth tithe barn, Gloucestershire*

dividing the intermediate bays. Also in Worcestershire is Bredon barn, which was built about 1350 for the bishops of Worcester, lords of the manor here for about 600 years. The building has been fully restored after being badly damaged by fire in 1980. Smaller than these but equally impressive is the one at Ashleworth in Gloucestershire, which forms part of a picturesque group of buildings on the banks of the River Severn. It was built in about 1500, probably by the canons of St Augustine's, Bristol, who were lords of the manor here.

All these barns were constructed of stone, but many others were built of timber. Leigh Court barn in Worcestershire was built by Pershore Abbey and is the best of those of cruck construction. Coggeshall Grange barn is the oldest timber-framed barn in England, having been built for the Savigniac monks of Coggeshall Abbey soon after the founding of the community in 1142. Although it was exten-

155 *Lenham tithe barn, Kent*

sively rebuilt in the late fourteenth century, the original aisle post still supports the roof. The most impressive group of timber-framed buildings, however, stands at Cressing Temple in Essex where the Barley Barn dates from between 1211 and 1220 and the Wheat Barn between 1273 and 1285. Both were built by the Knights Templars. The barns at Coggeshall and Cressing Temple are of aisle construction.

In Tudor times the landowners on their recently acquired land followed their monastic predecessors in the construction of imposing barns whose architectural quality belied their humble agricultural purpose. Nowhere can this be better seen than in Norfolk, where the landowners built a remarkable series of barns. The great brick one at Hales Court, built by James Hobart, Attorney General to Henry VII, at the end of the fifteenth century, the one at Paston, dated 1581, built by Sir William Paston, the one at Waxham and the one at Dersingham Hall, dated 1671, are perhaps the best. The largest is Hales Court at 184 feet (56 metres); the one at Paston is 163 feet (49.7 metres), the one at Waxham 161 feet (48.9 metres) and the one at Dersingham 98 feet (29.9 metres). Paston barn is very narrow – only 24 feet (7.3 metres) wide – and its steeply pitched roof, some 60 feet (18.3 metres) to the apex, adds to the impression of its enormous length. The one at Dersingham is the most decorative, and uses local materials: carstone to the gable ends, the 4 foot (1.2 metres) high plinth and the eaves band, with red brick dressings to quoins, openings and finally the crow-stepped gables. The tradition of barn-building continued in the county on the 'model' farms at Holkham (1790–2) and Leicester Square Farm, Syderstone (1791).

Smaller landowners and yeomen farmers also built barns, although they were much smaller and plainer than those built by the monasteries and larger landowners. The majority date from the seventeenth century and continued to be built until the last quarter of the nineteenth century. Generally they are of three bays, with a central threshing floor and the end bays used for storage. The overall length, however, can vary considerably. Traditional materials were used in the construction of these barns; in the south and east of England they were usually of timber, weatherboarded and tarred; elsewhere they were generally of stone beneath a timber roof, but, in those areas where there was little good timber or stone, other materials were used. Many barns were built of cob, not only in Devon and the South-west but elsewhere, for instance in Northamptonshire. In Buckinghamshire, around Haddenham, they were built of wychert, like one in Flint Street, and in southern Norfolk and the adjoining part of Suffolk clay-lump was widely used, often tarred to give it some protection. Brick was also used in Norfolk at an early stage, as at Old Hall, Colton, dated 1666, which incorporated crow-step gables, and Manor Farm, Kirby Bedon, dated 1693, with Dutch gables. Flint with brick dressings was widely used in Norfolk as elsewhere where flint was available.

Many of the medieval barns are often called tithe barns but the name is probably only correctly given to those built on ecclesiastical estates to house tithes.

Barns were primarily buildings for the storage and processing of corn, but there are many examples of ones which also housed cattle. In Yorkshire, for instance, it is believed that the wide aisles of some barns were used for cattle, and similar arrangements were certainly in use in Lancashire. Some barns in Surrey and Sussex also appeared to have housed cattle, but in much of south-east and eastern England aisled barns were only intended for corn. The bank-barns of the Lake District were essentially corn barns over a combined byre, cart shed and stable. They were built into the natural slope of the land or with an artificial mound against one side which provided direct access to the central threshing floor on the upper floor. Opposite the entrance, on the down side, was a winnowing door to provide a through draught. Trapdoors were provided in the floor in order that straw could be dropped to the cattle and horses below. The lower floor comprised a byre and a stable flanking a cart shed with access on the lower side.

In 1788 Andrew Meikle patented the threshing machine and the mechanization of the process brought at first rapid change and then sudden obsolescence to many barns. The early threshing machines, which were mostly driven by horses or occasionally by water power, could easily be fitted into the traditional barn. In some areas in the early nineteenth century, particularly in Northumberland, a wheelhouse, known as a gin-gang, was constructed next to the barn to house a wheel turned by a horse, the power being transferred by a shaft to the threshing machine. In the mid-nineteenth century steam power came, to the farm and to this day factory-type chimneys which were built to serve this new form of power can still be seen on some of our farms. However, steam power did not last long for portable threshing machines, hauled and driven by steam engines, proved more conven-ient and so over the years more corn was threshed outside and less in the barn. Barns ceased to be built and existing ones were gradually adapted to other purposes or allowed to degenerate into storage areas.

Recently, like other redundant buildings, many ancient barns have been converted to domestic use and, like other historical buildings, need careful adaptation if many of the architectural and historical details are not to be lost.

Granaries

 ⌒

Grain was, without doubt, the most precious and carefully guarded farm produce. Not only did it provide the essential ingredients for bread and ale, but also the seeds from which the following year's crop was grown, as well as the main cash crop. At first grain yields were small and, because of its value and comparatively small bulk, it was kept in the farmhouse, perhaps in the attic.

In the eighteenth and nineteenth centuries, with increased yields, purpose built granaries, which could be kept both locked and guarded, became common. They were small, rectangular structures, normally raised above the ground on mushroom-shaped stone supports called staddle stones, which provided protection from vermin and dampness. Staddle stones are most sought after, and can often be seen as garden ornaments. Some granaries were raised to first-floor level above an open cart shed or perhaps a stable. The most famous and largest example is at Peper Harow Farm in Surrey, which stands like a market hall, surrounded by farm buildings and cottages. The upper storey, supported on twenty-five massive posts, is tile-hung and probably dates from the eighteenth century, but the timber posts and framing have been dated to about 1600. Raised granaries often incorporated dog kennels, usually below the stairs, to protect the corn against thieves. This can be seen at the combined granary and cart shed re-erected at the Avoncroft Museum of Buildings at Stoke Prior in Worcestershire. Because of the value of the grain, granaries were well constructed, the interior plastered or boarded throughout and the floors plastered or fitted with rebated boards.

Most granaries are to be found in the grain-growing areas of southern and eastern England, but today they are seldom used for their original purpose. Combine harvesters and complicated multi-purpose grain-drying, cleaning and storage units have rendered them obsolete, but many remain on modern farms and are used as useful stores for seeds, fertilizers and tools.

Cattle Buildings

Cattle have always been important to the English farm system, whether for dairy production, meat, with leather as a by-product, ploughing and carting, or producing manure for crops.

Climate is the major factor in cattle husbandry. Although most stock could be put out to graze during the summer, in most areas over-wintering in the fields was not feasible because of the damage done to the grassland by cattle in wet weather. They were therefore brought in during the winter, dairy cows and working oxen usually being tethered in stalls or kept in a foldyard, open to the weather and protected by the surrounding buildings, or in open-fronted shelter sheds which they could enter at will. These shelter sheds could be freestanding or form part of a range of buildings on the side of the foldyard, usually as a lean-to against a barn. In some areas, particularly Devon, an open-fronted hay-storage loft was provided above the shelter sheds to form a building known as a linhay.

Straw, in its various forms, played an important part in cattle husbandry, not only as fodder but also for litter. When mixed with dung and trodden and compacted by the animals' hoofs, it was returned to the fields as manure. In the highland zone, because of the lack of straw and the high rainfall, foldyards are seldom found. The cattle were housed in a byre which formed part of a longhouse, a laithe, a field-house or a bank-barn in winter and put to pasture in summer. Longhouses, in which house and byre were under one roof but separated by a through-passage running across the building, are mostly found along the western fringe of the highland zone in the south-west of England, the Welsh Marches and the Lake District. Laithes are a type of barn specifically designed for cattle and are common in the Pennines, where there is a predominance of cattle over grain. The term laithe means a combined byre and barn, and they could well incorporate stables and cart bays as well as hay lofts and granaries above. Sometimes the house was attached to the laithe and was known as a laithe-house. They differ from longhouses in that they have no through-passage and usually no connecting door between house and laithe. Throughout much of the highland zone it is common for houses and farm buildings to be joined together in line and laithe-houses may be a special instance of a more general pattern. They are to be found in the Yorkshire Pennines. The field-house is characteristic of upland pastoral farming. It comprises a two-storeyed building, usually on a sloping site some distance from the farmstead, in which hay from the surrounding meadows is stored above and fed to the cattle below. The Cumbrian equivalent of the field-house is the bank-barn.

The historical importance of cattle to English farming is not reflected in the buildings that have survived. There are two reasons for this: first, the simple shed shelters were often poorly constructed and have collapsed or been demolished; and secondly, because of the ever-increasing demands of hygiene and convenience in milk production, most have been replaced with new, improved milk parlours.

Stables

Before the coming of the tractor farmers depended on horse power, so good stabling was important. Today we associate stables with horses but for many centuries oxen were also used; only in Victorian times did horses start to replace them. In the Cotswolds and Sussex they continued to be used for some farm work until the early part of the last century. Horses were expensive and stables were often well constructed to provide good, clean accommodation with single, wide stalls and hay lofts above. Provision was also made for harnesses, either hung on a wall opposite the stalls or in a separate tack-room. Today teams of horses are no more than a memory, revived from time to time at local shows and ploughing matches, and with them the stables have also gone. Some have been demolished, others converted to other uses.

Horses were not only used on the farms, but for centuries provided the main means of transport, whether for haulage, for riding, or for pulling carriages or traps. Stables were therefore provided in many villages and many houses had stables for one or two horses and often a small carriage house. These can still be seen, often converted into a store or garage.

Cart and Implement Sheds

Wagons, carts, ploughs and harrows were all expensive pieces of equipment and it was therefore necessary to provide shelter to protect them from the worst of the weather, for being made substantially of timber they were liable to rot and warp, while the iron moving parts would rust and seize up.

The sheds provided to house this equipment were the simplest of all the buildings of the farmstead, often being no more than an open-fronted or open-ended building, seldom fitted with any doors. As with granaries and stables, most date from the eighteenth and nineteenth centuries. In some cases rooms were provided over the cart shed, most commonly for use as a granary, but sometimes to store hand tools, paints and spare parts.

Dovecotes

Before animals were over-wintered, pigeons were kept to provide fresh meat over the winter period, and special buildings were built to house them. In medieval times the right to keep pigeons was a feudal privilege restricted to the barons, abbots and lords of the manor, with the privilege later extended to parish priests. Subsequently the restrictions were further relaxed; by the seventeenth century it has been estimated that there were 26,000 dovecotes and a century or so later no farmstead would have been complete without one. By 1800, however, there were so many that a tax was proposed on them in an attempt to reduce the loss of grain; the birds not only ate the owner's grain but also that of his neighbours. By this time, however, the keeping of pigeons was in decline and no legislation was introduced.

Although many dovecotes have been lost plenty of excellent examples still remain, and the use of local materials, changing architectural trends, and preferences in size and shape have resulted in a great variety of regional designs. Stone, timber-framing, either exposed or clad with plaster and weatherboarding, and later brick were all used in their construction.

The earliest dovecotes, constructed of rubble stone, were cylindrical with a conical roof. At Dunster in Somerset there is a fine example, which is believed to have been built by a Norman baron at the time of William the Conqueror, but which was altered

156 *Dovecote, Dunster, Somerset*

157 *Dovecote, Norton sub Hamdon, Somerset*

by Benedictine monks in the twelfth century and later reroofed, probably more than once. The one at Quenington Court in Gloucestershire dates from the thirteenth century, and is all that remains of an establishment which once belonged to the Knights Templar. The one in the churchyard at Norton sub Hamdon in Somerset is also of interest, being originally attached to the manor house but later enclosed when the churchyard was extended.

Generally of a later date are the numerous square and rectangular dovecotes. Normally these are simple buildings, but in Gloucestershire they frequently have four gables with cupolas at the intersection of the ridges and gables. One excellent example stands in the village of Naunton; it once belonged to the manor house and was at one time converted for use as a watermill. It has been restored and is now looked after by the local Dovecote Society.

One of the most spectacular dovecotes is at Willington in Bedfordshire. Built by Sir John Goshawk, Cardinal Wolsey's Master of Horse, in 1530, it is now owned by the National Trust. It is notable for its crow-stepped gables and the roof, which resembles the so-called lectern type found only in Scotland and parts of France. Most of the early square and rectangular dovecotes are of stone but later ones are of brick or timber. Most are to be found in the West Midlands, and those at Hawford Grange and Wichenford Court in Worcestershire are

158 *Dovecote, Hawford Grange, Worcestershire*

excellent examples from the seventeenth century. They now belong to the National Trust. The one at Moat Farm, Dormston, also in Worcestershire, is owned and was restored by the Avoncroft Museum of Buildings which also owns the sole surviving cruck-frame dovecote in the country at Glebe Farm, Hill Croome, Worcestershire. Another recently restored example stands at Luntley Court, Dilwyn, Herefordshire. Timber-framed dovecotes were also common in Essex and Suffolk but few remain; one example is to be found at Great Yeldham in Essex.

Square and rectangular dovecotes were replaced by hexagonal or octagonal ones. Although some continued to be built of stone many were constructed of brick. They were often plain, but recessed panels, diaper patterns in contrasting bricks, dentil courses and saw-tooth cornices were all typical embellishments. A combination of brick and stone was also used, and flint, as at the one at New Timber Place, West Sussex, is most pleasing.

There was a general decline in the use of dovecotes towards the end of the eighteenth century, although new ones continued to be built. Many were designed with few architectural pretensions, but during the eighteenth century their ornamental aspect was exploited, some becoming features in the new landscaped gardens, and some achieved sufficient architectural and historical merit to be classified as scheduled buildings. One striking example is at Barrington Park in Gloucestershire, where the dovecote and stables, built in the form of a classical temple, are a focal point in the grounds.

Dovecotes were not the only buildings built to house pigeons. Lofts were often used, normally in farm buildings, particularly barns. One or two rows of holes in one of the gables, each with a small landing platform, provided access to an area within the roof space. This arrangement is particularly common in many barns in the southern Cotswolds. Alternatively rows of nesting boxes were provided in the external face of one of the gables, each row with a continuous landing platform. Again, this arrangement can be found not only on barns but also on dwellings like the cottages at Mansell Lacey, Herefordshire, and Aynho, Northamptonshire.

Like so many other redundant buildings, some have been put to other uses, mainly as garden stores, but a few of the larger ones have been converted into habitable dwellings, the large square ones being most suitable for this purpose. The spacious Dutch-gabled dovecote at

Wolverley in Worcestershire and the seventeenth-century timber-framed one at Great Shelford, Cambridgeshire, are two excellent examples.

Oast-houses

Oast-houses or hop-kilns were brick or stone buildings each of which contained a kiln for drying hops before they were used in the brewery industry. They are to be found in hop-growing areas of Kent, East Sussex, Herefordshire and the western part of Worcestershire. Hops were introduced into this country by Flemish weavers in the fourteenth century, but were not grown here to any great extent until the sixteenth century when it was realized that they could replace wormwood as a preservative to stop beer from souring.

Unlike the process of preparing barley for brewing, which was generally carried out in separate industrial buildings some distance away, hops were usually dried on the farm. The oast-houses that survive today are square or circular, with characteristic tall pyramidal or conical roofs surmounted by a wooden ventilation cowl driven round by a windvane, and were built in the nineteenth century. Early kilns were square and were attached to or built into a barn or even formed a wing of the farmhouse. It was not until the beginning of the nineteenth century that the attractive circular oasts began to appear in Kent (Court Lodge Farm, Brook, has one dated 1815), soon spreading into Sussex before reaching Herefordshire some time after 1835. Square ones reappeared in the Herefordshire area in the 1870s but were not used in Kent and Sussex until much later. The furnace was usually in the lower part of the oast-house, with the drying floor above, on which the hops were spread with the hot air from below passing through them.

Attached to the oast-house was a two-storeyed building. The upper floor was used for spreading the hops out to cool after they had been removed from the drying room prior to packing. Hops needed to be packed tightly if they were to keep; pockets, long sacks into which the hops were packed, were suspended through a circular hole in the floor, known as the treading hole. Until presses were intro-duced they were compressed by a man, known as a bagger, treading them in. The lower floor was only used to stoke the fires, provide space for the pockets to hang and provide storage for filled pockets prior to collection.

Like so many agricultural processes, the drying of hops has radically changed; they are now dried with electric heaters and, like so many agricultural buildings, oast-houses have become redundant. They are now used for storage or have been converted into houses.

SEVEN

Miscellanea

There are several small buildings and other objects, often referred to as street furniture, which add interest and character to many of our villages. Most of them are, or have been in the past, public structures but much, particularly street furniture, has been a target for change as the villages come to terms with modern needs. There is still much to see, however, for what has survived is looked after and treasured by local inhabitants. Some are to be found only in certain locations, for instance the literary institutes of Swaledale, North Yorkshire, of which the one at Muker is the finest.

Guide-posts and Milestones

Milestones were known in Roman times, but it was not until the reign of Charles II that they once again began to make their appearance along England's main roads. Mile marks were provided in 1663 on the Dover road and on the Great North Road in 1708. However, the first true milestone to be set up in England since Roman times was in 1717 at Trumpington, Cambridgeshire, where it can still be seen. It is one of a series, most of which survive, along what was, in the eighteenth century, the main road from Cambridge to London. Most early milestones were

159 *Literary institute, Muker, North Yorkshire*

the result of private enterprise and they did not become compulsory until 1773, when all turnpike trusts were required to provide them on their roads. Each trust was impelled to 'cause to be fixed, in the most convenient Place where .... ways meet, a Stone or Post with an inscription thereon in Large Letters, containing the Name of, and Distance from, the next Market Town or Towns, or other considerable Places or Place to which the said Highways respectively lead'.

Guide-posts of a kind, in the form of wayside crosses, were often used in medieval England, often set up by religious houses to guide travellers across the featureless moors in the Peak District and Dartmoor. Later, guide-stones were provided on the rough tracks on these wild and lonely moors, bearing the name of the next town or village. It was not until the end of the seventeenth century, however, that new sign-posts began to be erected when, in 1698, an act required justices to erect standing-posts at crossroads. Like so many acts, however, it seems to have had little effect and they did not become common until they became compulsory in the act of 1773. Although most milestones and sign-posts date from after this act there are a few which pre-date it. One of the earliest surviving ones is the one at Fish Hill, Broadway, Worcestershire, which was provided by a local farmer, Nathan Izod, in 1669, its wooden post carrying four metal arms, each terminating in a roughly shaped hand pointing the directions with the mileage to Woster, Gloster, Warwick and Oxford. Another is at Withington, Herefordshire. Erected in 1700 and made from the shaft of an old cross, it gives one the not very useful information, that 'this is the road to Hereford'. At Hopton, Derbyshire, is a post dated 1705, while at Bicton, in Devon, is a fine brick pillar, dated 1743, with directions and scriptural texts on its four sides.

Early sign-posts and mile-stones were usually obelisks standing several feet high for the convenience of travellers on horse-back or in coaches. Many, like those at Bredon, Worcestershire, and Nayland, Suffolk, have no indication in which direction the various places named are to be

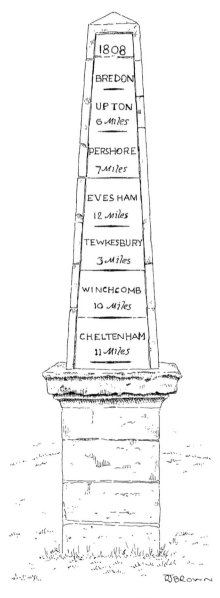

160 *Milestone, Bredon, Worcestershire*

found. These early milestones were usually of stone, but in Victorian times cast-iron ones of various shapes became common, usually painted white with the lettering in black.

Monuments

∽

Monuments are to be found in many parts of the country. They are nearly always erected to commemorate an event, such as a birth, a death or a battle, and usually take the form of a stone cross, obelisk or pillar. The most common, and found in most villages, are war memorials erected in honour of those who fell in the two world wars. They are usually found in the churchyard, at a crossroads or on the village green. Usually erected by public subscription they take the form of a stone cross mounted on a stepped base, bearing on each of its sides an engraved list of those who died in the service of their country. One of the finest is to be found at Briantspuddle, Dorset. Carved by Eric Gill, it consists of a tall cross with a life-sized statue of the wounded Christ on the north side and a Madonna and Child beneath a canopy on the south. Another good example is at Slaidburn in Lancashire, with a statue of a solider, head bent, on top of an octagonal pillar.

161 *Domed memorial, Delly End, Oxfordshire*

At Geddington, Northamptonshire, near the church and at the meeting point of three roads, stands a cross erected by Edward I to mark the overnight resting place of Queen Eleanor's coffin as it was carried on its way from Harby, Nottinghamshire, where she died in November 1290, to Westminster Abbey, where she was buried. Of the twelve crosses which originally marked the stopping places, only three now remain; in addition to the one at Geddington, they are at Hardingstone, near Northampton and at Waltham Cross, Hertfordshire. The one at Geddington is the most perfectly preserved, having a triangular shaft with the three statues of a veiled Eleanor.

To the south of Finedon, Northamptonshire, by the A510, is a circular stone tower with a central chimney and balcony. Known as the Round House, it was erected by General Arbuthnot of Woodford House after the Duke of Wellington had stayed with him and found that the local landscape, when viewed from the tower's site, resembled the terrain in which the Battle of Waterloo was fought. He had the tower erected to commemorate both the duke's visit and the battle. A sunken cross-shaped plaque on the side reads: 'Panarama, Waterloo Victory, June AD 1815'.

Wells, Conduits, Standpipes and Drinking Fountains

Fresh water is one of life's essentials and the importance of a reliable source to the village's wellbeing cannot be overstated. It was not, however, until the second half of the twentieth century that many villages received piped water, and even today numerous remote farm-houses and cottages still depend upon natural sources. Those who did not have their own private supply had to rely on a public source which might be a spring, a well, a conduit, a pump, a standpipe or a drinking fountain. These were often situated some distance away and the purity of the water itself was often questionable. Many of these sources still survive, particularly village pumps, but few are still in working order.

At first water was supplied by a stream which the villagers shared with their livestock, with little regard for hygiene. Wells have been used as a source of water from medieval times and 'well' is incorporated in many village names. Early wells would have been formed of under-ground water which rose spontaneously to the surface. They are often found in the West Country and in the upland villages of the Pennines, where the distribution of springs is determined by geological factors. Many were regarded as holy, and are often located close by the church. Stevington in Bedfordshire has a 'Holy Well' set in a recess in the boundary wall of the churchyard, which was a place of pilgrimage in the Middle Ages. As late as the nineteenth century it was being used for sheep-dipping. As with so many ancient wells the spring which still feeds it has never been known to freeze or run dry. Others of note are St Winifred's well at Woolston in Shropshire, which is said to have sprung miraculously from the ground after St Winifred had rested there for a night in 1138. Cornwall has a number of holy wells; those at Luxulyan and Dupath Well House, near Callington, are of special interest.

162 *Holy well, Luxulyan, Cornwall*

The five wells at Tissington in Derbyshire have never failed to supply water, even in 1615 when '… no rayne fell upon the earth from 25th day of March to the second day of May and then there was but one shower. Two more fell between then and the 4th day of August, so that the greatest part of the land was burnt up…' Today Tissington is known as the mother place of well-dressing in Derbyshire; it is now an annual event.

Where no surface water was available villagers were obliged to dig wells. Today they are not particularly common, for their deep shafts were a danger to children and animals and many were filled in when a village pump or piped water was supplied. In the nineteenth century well-heads were often provided to protect the operating gear as well as those drawing off the water. Many are utilitarian but others are far more pretentious. Notable examples are to be found on the village green at Preston in Hertfordshire, which still has its operating gear, and on the common at Abinger, Surrey. The latter was erected by William John Evelyn, lord of the manor, and was 'declared open for use of Abinger Parishioners August 11th 1895'. At Aldworth in Berkshire is another particularly fine example, its two-tiered tiled roof supported on wooden posts, giving it an air of importance as it stands at the village crossroads. At 372 feet (113.4 metres) deep, is reputedly the deepest well in England.

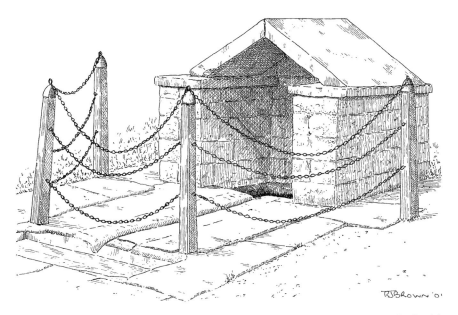

163 *Town Well, Tissington, Derbyshire*

Perhaps the most extraordinary well is the Maharajah's Well at Stoke Row, Oxfordshire, the result of the close relationship between the Maharajah of Benares and a local resident, Edward Anderton Reade, who served in India for over thirty-four years. Built in 1864 the cast-iron structure is crowned by a gilt elephant and surmounted by a Mughal dome. A far more substantial building is the wellhouse and clock tower on Heath Green, Heath and Reach, Bedfordshire, which was erected by subscription in 1873. The cost of the clock was borne by Baroness Burdett Coutts and Baroness de Rothschild, while the pump was presented by Mr Branton in memory of William Abraham. Through the iron grilles of the wheelhouse can still be seen the 4 foot (1.2 metres) diameter wheel used to raise the water.

Where there was no water supply an artificial watercourse was provided, in the form of either a culvert or pipes, which ran from the source to a position within the village, often finishing with a conduit head. The finest perhaps is to be found at Little Walsingham in Norfolk, which probably dates from around 1530. It is octagonal, built of brick with stone dressings and a truncated stone pyramid roof from which the original pinnacle fell in 1900; what was salvaged was re-erected. The conduit head is now capped with a brazier used for celebratory fires. Another, built around 1550 on the green at Long Melford, Suffolk, was constructed by

Sir William Cordell to supply water to his newly built Melford Hall and the village. Of slightly later date, probably seventeenth century, is the one at Hallaton, Leicestershire. Not so ornate as the one at Little Walsingham, it is a simple, box-like structure with a pitched roof more like a little shrine. Another conduit of nineteenth-century date is to be found in the square at Youlgreave, Derbyshire. Known locally as The Fountain, it was erected in 1829 to house water for the village via a conduit from springs in the Dales.

Pumps, which first appeared in the eighteenth century, were at first manufactured locally and were often of rudimentary construction, made with lead pipes and spouts. Following the industrial revolution, cast-iron pumps began to be provided, often to replace earlier open wells. Most dated from the nineteenth century and in particular after the introduction of the Public Health (Water) Act of 1878, which required all new rural housing to be built with its own water supply. Typical is the one to be found on the village green at Comberton, Cambridgeshire. Some pumps had two spouts, the lower one

164 *Conduit Head, Little Walsingham, Norfolk*

165 *Conduit head, Long Melford, Suffolk*

domestic use, the upper one for such purposes as filling the tanks of traction engines, water carts and horse-drawn fire-engine bowsers. These pumps can stand some 8 feet (2.4 metres) high. A good example still remains at Preston Candover in Hampshire.

166 *The Fountain, Youlgreave, Derbyshire*

These exposed pumps were often encased in wood as a protection against frost. In most instances the covering was purely practical, consisting of simple boarding, as at Kersey, Suffolk, but in a few cases they were elaborately carved. The one at Haynes Church End, Bedfordshire, is particularly fine, with its spout in the form of a medieval gargoyle. Cast iron was a popular material in Victorian times and many pumps were erected with an ornamental casing. The village pump on the green at Monks Eleigh in Suffolk tells its own story, having the inscription 'This well was made and pump erected 1854 for use of the inhabitants of Monks Eleigh out of the proceeds of the sale of some parish property. Joseph Makin Guardian of the Poor.'

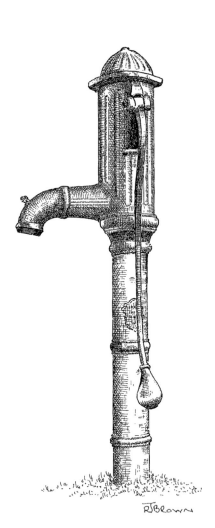

167 *Cast-iron hand pump, Comberton, Cambridgeshire*

168 *Village pump, Kersey, Suffolk*

169 *Village pump, Monks Eleigh, Suffolk*

With the increased use of cast iron, pumps became more elaborate and often bore the name of the benefactor; the one at Earls Colne in Essex is typical, erected in 1853 by Mary Gee, a local benefactor, 'in thankful commemoration for the absence of cholera' and known locally as the Cholera Pump.

Like well-heads, pumps were often protected by a canopy. Most were simple structures but others were more elaborate, and often erected by a benefactor. The pump at Haynes Church End, Bedfordshire, is protected by a large wooden structure with a decorative tiled roof, the whole put up in about 1867 by Lord John Thynne. No doubt its attractive appearance is due to the fact that it stands opposite the entrance to what was his country house, Haynes Park.

Where there was a suitable water supply, standpipes and drinking fountains were erected. These were frequently manufactured by Glenfield and Kennedy of Kilmarnock, who supplied cast-iron standpipes and drinking fountains throughout Britain. Standpipes, from which the villagers were allowed to draw off water using a turn key, were often simple affairs, like those found at Aveton Gifford in Devon. The ones at Nenthead, Cumbria, and

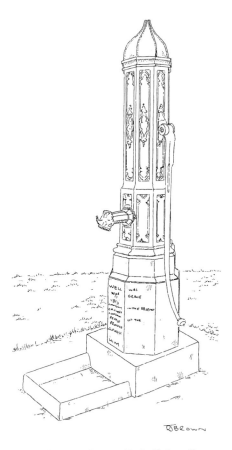

170 *Cholera Pump, Earls Colne, Essex*

171 *Village pump, Haynes Church End, Bedfordshire*

172 *Village pump, Wyck Rissington, Gloucestershire*

173 *Drinking fountain, horse and dog trough, Grasmere, Cumbria*

174 *Drinking fountain, Slaidburn, Lancashire*

Middleton-in-Teesdale, Country Durham, have ornate cast-iron canopies over a commonplace standpipe. Both the standpipes and canopies were cast by Glenfield and Kennedy. The one at Middleton-in-Teesdale is mounted with a boy sitting on a dophin.

Drinking fountains became a popular source of water in the nineteenth century, particularly in northern England where they are known as 'pants'. They are generally simple structures, unlike the ornate ones seen in towns. Memorial drinking fountains were often erected, some to the famous and some to the not so famous; at Grasmere in Cumbria there is a simple drinking fountain, horse and dog trough erected as a memorial to William Wordsworth in 1889 and engraved with a verse from one of his sonnets. Some were erected to commemorate one of Queen Victoria's jubilees, like those at Slaidburn in Lancashire and Sedbergh, Cumbria, both erected to celebrate the Diamond Jubilee of 1887.

Stocks, Whipping Posts and Pillories

Stocks were an important feature of village life, and these symbols of public humiliation are still to be found on village greens, close by village crosses, or sometimes in churchyards (in a few instances they have even found their way into the church). It was in 1381, following the Statute of Labourers, that every village was ordered by Edward III to provide and maintain a set of stocks for the punishment of offenders. As a form of punishment, they lasted for some 500 years, the last recorded use being in 1865. Today, they are often treasured possessions, sometimes protected from the worst of the weather under a tiled canopy, like those at Witham on the Hill, Lincolnshire, and Apethorpe, Northamptonshire. Many are not as old as they appear, often being replicas of ancient ones, but a few are obviously of great age, such as the one on the village green at Aldbury in Hertfordshire. Most are of timber, but in some stone-bearing areas they were often partly or wholly constructed of stone. Occasionally they were formed entirely of iron; one such stands at Painswick, Gloucestershire, known locally as the Squire's Spectacles, and another at Ninfield, East Sussex.

175 *Iron stocks, Painswick, Gloucestershire*

176 *Village stocks, Aldbury, Hertfordshire*

Another instance of the barbarous side of old village life are whipping posts attached to the stocks. They have iron clamps by which the offender was held by his wrists while he was flogged. These can be seen on the stocks at Aldbury and Brent Pelham, both in Hertfordshire, and the iron one at Ninfield.

Close by the stocks or as part of them, one sometimes finds a pillory, a frame with holes, in which the head and hands of the evil-doer were held fast while the villagers threw missiles (rotten eggs and vegetables) at him. One surviving example is the eighteenth century one at Coleshill, Warwickshire, where the culprit was made to stand on a raised platform.

Lock-ups

Prior to the establishment of a properly constituted police force in 1856, it was the duty of each parish to elect an unpaid petty constable whose responsibility, amongst others, was the apprehension and detention of suspected criminals, drunks and trouble-makers. To hold these people, a lock-up or cage was provided. Those committing a misdemeanour were detained overnight, while those committing a felony were held pending their removal to court.

Surviving lock-ups are not uncommon and can easily be identified by their barred window openings and heavy ironwork to the doors. Most are cramped, single-cell affairs but occasionally two cells were provided so that both sexes could be housed when necessary;

177 *Lock-up, Kingsbury Episcopi, Somerset*

one notable example is at Bisley in Gloucestershire, dated 1824. Many that survive are substantial buildings dating from between 1750 and 1830. Those in stone-bearing areas are mainly hexagonal, octagonal, as at Kingsbury Episcopi, Somerset, or cylindrical with a domed top. The most unusual is the one at Wheatley, Oxfordshire, which is pyramidal. The stone lock-up at Steeple Ashton in Wiltshire is octagonal, with an octagonal domed roof mounted with a finial.

Outside the stone-bearing areas most lock-ups were simple, rectangular brick structures with a slate or tiled roof resembling nothing more than a shed. However, there are some of interest, like the one at Bradwell-on-Sea in Essex, built in 1817 at a cost of £3 10s 9d, which retains some old restraining irons. The one at Great Bardfield, also in Essex, was built of brick and flint and is open to the public. At Shenley, Hertfordshire, the lock-up is cylindrical with a domed roof, the whole building being rendered. Rather more ambitious brick lock-ups were constructed in the Midlands; the ones at Packington and Worthington, both in

178 *Lock-up, Wheatley, Oxfordshire*

179 *Lock-up, Shenley, Hertfordshire*

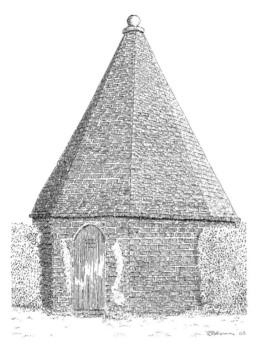

180 *Lock-up, Packington, Leicestershire*

182 *Lock-up, Deeping St James, Lincolnshire*

181 *Lock-up, Barley, Hertfordshire*

Leicestershire, are octagonal with octagonal pointed roofs. Derbyshire has two similar octagonal structures, one at Smisby and the other at Ticknall. In those areas where timber-framing was prevalent, a few survive; the one at Tollesbury in Essex is little more than a weatherboarded shed but at Barley in Hertfordshire there is a substantial timber-framed structure.

Not all lock-ups were specially constructed; sometimes existing buildings were used. At Stratton, Cornwall, the south porch of the church was used, at Thaxted, Essex, a lock-up was built within the ground floor of the guildhall, while at Anstey, Hertfordshire, part of the fifteenth-century lych-gate was converted in the nineteenth century. Perhaps the most unusual is to be found at Deeping St James in Lincolnshire where the medieval cross was converted.

Another lock-up of interest is to be found at Lingfield, Surrey, where St Peter's Cross, erected in 1473 to mark the boundaries between neighbouring manors, had a lock-up attached to it in 1773. It was last used in 1882, for detaining poachers. The top of the cross is now missing.

183 *St Peter's Cross and lock-up, Lingfield, Surrey*

Pinfolds

The agricultural equivalent of the lock-up was the pinfold or pound. Sometimes as at Sandiacre, Derbyshire, which according to the plaque was erected in about 1660, and at Clophill in Bedfordshire, it was combined with the lock-up. The number of horses, cattle, hogs, sheep or geese to which each tenant farmer was entitled was carefully scheduled, and cases of encroachment, trespass or excess were jealously noted. Strays or unauthorized intruders were vigorously impounded and held until a fine was paid. Most medieval villages had a pound in which these stray animals could be kept. It was usually maintained by the lord of the manor and was the responsibility of a pinder or pound-reeve, a minor official. Laxton, Nottinghamshire, is the only village in England to retain its medieval strip-farming system, for three fields have never been enclosed. Even now the Court Leet meets every 23

184 *Pinfold and lock-up, Sandiacre, Derbyshire*

November to administer the annual leases of these fields (some 483 acres, 195 ha) and appoint a pinder to impound any stray animals in the village pinfold.

Most medieval pounds would have been built of perishable wooden fencing or hurdles, but later more substantial structures of brick or stone were provided on the sites of the medieval ones. Some of these have survived, particularly in the Midlands, where the open fields were enclosed later than in most areas. Many villages in Nottinghamshire still retain their pinfolds. The one at Laxton has already been mentioned and those at East Markham, Epperstone and Scarrington are typical, but the one at Norwell is unusual in being circular and built of brick. It dates from the late eighteenth or early nineteenth century. At Hutton-le-Hole, North Yorkshire, there is also a circular pinfold, but built of stone. The most unusual one to survive is at Raskelf, North Yorkshire, which is an open crenellated polygon with arched and barred door and window openings.

After the enclosures pounding became obsolete and pinfolds soon fell into disrepair and many have disappeared, but their former presence is remembered in many villages by names such as Pound or Pinfold Lane.

Bier-houses

Most villages owned a bier, a three- or four-wheeled (usually hand-propelled but later sometimes horse-drawn) carriage on which a coffin was transported to the church. Many were, and still are, housed in the church, others with the local coffin-maker but a few were kept in a bier-house. Few now survive; probably the finest is the stone structure built into the boundary wall at the village church of Beckington in Somerset. It is little more than a scaled-down version of a normal-sized carriage-house with doors no more than 3 feet (90cm) high. Many are little more than sheds, like the brick and tiled one in Cambridgeshire by the roadside at Wilburton cemetery. Another stands at Cople in Bedfordshire; because of a change in land-ownership, it now stands on the front lawn of a modern house. Built in the late nineteenth century it has been restored with the help of a grant from the County council.

185 *Bier house, Cople, Bedfordshire*

Fire-engine Houses

Fire was a particular hazard in areas where timber-framed or thatched buildings were common. Before the days of local-authority fire brigades, insurance companies maintained their own fire engines. To prevent the wrong company being called out, many houses had on the wall a large metal plaque showing with which company the house was insured. These fire-marks are still to be found on old buildings. Later, individual parishes took control of fire-fighting and often provided small buildings to house either hand- or horse-drawn engines. Most were simple structures, generally dating from the early part of the nineteenth century, and often with no distinguishing features, so people passing by are unaware of their former importance. Some are more easily recognizable, like the one at Melbourne in Cambridgeshire, which is clearly signed 'Melbourne Fire Engine'. Many are rather drab-looking buildings but not the one at Singleton in Lancashire, which is of a black-and-white design perhaps more characteristic of Cheshire than Lancashire.

186 *Fire-engine house, Singleton, Lancashire*

Bakehouses

~

Bread was the staple food of the villagers and, although some larger villages supported a baker, most bread was baked at home in a brick oven beside the fire. In a few instances a communal bakehouse was provided. The one at Averham, Nottinghamshire, is a small brick building with a stable door and a chimney at the back. On the small green at Papworth St Agnes, Cambridgeshire, is another, dating from about the middle of the nineteenth century and built of local white gault bricks with a slated roof and, at the west end, a tall industrial chimney. The interior, which, apart from baking dough, is said to have been used also for scalding pigs, has been altered and the ovens long since removed. Another is to be found in the charming village of Aldbury, Hertfordshire. Timber-framed with a tiled roof, this small structure is said to date from the sixteenth century, although the tall octagonal chimney is thought to be Victorian.

187 *Bakehouse, Papworth St Agnes, Cambridgeshire*

Mounting Blocks

~

Mounting blocks, like horse troughs and tethering posts, are reminders of a lost horse-orientated age. Of stone, brick or timber, they were provided to assist the not so agile, or women with long skirts, to mount and dismount their horses and for those ascending

188 *Mounting block, Bradwell-on-Sea, Essex*

the high steps of a carriage or stagecoach.

Although they are now obsolete there are still a number to be seen, often close by the church or the inn. The majority of those that survive today are of stone, although brick and even timber were also used. Those of timber have generally disappeared but there is one outside the church at Epping Upland in Essex, which is formed of two steps and a platform and steadying post. A brick one stands beside the church at Fairfield in Kent.

Because of their utilitarian nature, they are difficult to date; among the few that are dated is a two-step one at Aston le Walls in Northamptonshire, which carries the inscription 'Thomas Height of Warden set this up July the 30 1659.' Most mounting blocks have the steps on one side only but occasionally steps are provided at both ends, as with the one near the church at Lowther in Cumbria. Perhaps the finest mounting block, still with its steadying post, stands at Bradwell-on-Sea in Essex.

Fives Walls

In medieval times a ball game known as fives was popular. A large, smooth wall was required, the game involving hitting a ball against it, and in most cases the only suitable wall in the village was on the church tower. It originated from the Spanish game pelota and is said to have been brought over to this country by monks. The idea was to hit the ball against the wall between the string courses and as the ball returned hit it again and so on. The higher the ball went the higher the score. There are many reports of fives being played in the churchyard, but the damage caused to the church structure and the rowdy behaviour of the players led to the church authorities banning the game in the eighteenth century.

In most areas, it seems, it was then abandoned but, in Somerset, inns became the new venues. Large fives walls, or towers as they were called, were built in the yards of the inns. One of the finest is at the Fleur-de-Lis in Stoke sub Hamdon. At the rear of the inn, it is some 45 feet (13.7 metres) high and 20 feet (6.1 metres) wide,

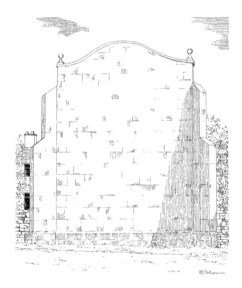

189 *Fives wall, Stoke sub Hamdon, Somerset*

supported at each end with buttresses with the top curved and capped with a stone coping. At each end there is a finial. Similar walls can be seen at the Poulett Arms at Hinton St George and in the garden of a bungalow at South Petherton, which originally formed part of the Crown Hotel. The game became much more sophisticated than when it was played against the church wall. The aim of the game was to spin the ball onto the tower so that it landed back onto a 6 foot (1.8 metre) square stone, known as the hopping stone, and when this was done a point was scored. The referee, or caller, nominated which part of the wall was to be hit. The game appears to have died out when skittles became popular.

Letterboxes

Letterboxes were first introduced in the British Isles in St Helier, Jersey, in 1852 and on the mainland the following year. Today they are a common feature in our villages, some as free-standing pillar boxes, others as wall boxes or lamp boxes, so called because they were originally intended to be fixed to lamp-posts, although they are frequently attached to telegraph poles or even embedded in walls.

From their inception it has been customary for most letterboxes to carry the royal cipher, which can assist in dating them. A number of manufacturers were employed by the Post Office to produce them and a number of unusual or rare examples, dating from the mid-nineteenth century, remain in use, although these are usually to be found in towns. One at Barnes Cross, Holwell, Dorset, dates from 1853–6 and is one of the only two known to exist.

Many letterboxes in villages are of the wall type, which was first introduced in 1858 as a cheaper alternative to the free-standing pillar boxes. Built either into the side of a wall or into a brick or stone pillar, they remain in use in country areas to this day. Probably the most attractive are the two at Rous Lench, Worcestershire, built in Tudor style with tiled roofs in 1876 by the Revd. W.K.W. Chafy outside the gates of Rous Lench Court. At Nether Winchendon in Buckinghamshire the wall-type box, made by the Eagle Foundry of Birmingham between 1871 and 1881, is contained in a large, stone rounded pillar topped by a pinnacle surmounted by an iron ball.

190 *Letterbox, Rous Lench, Worcestershire*

191 *Letterbox, Nether Winchendon, Buckinghamshire*

Telephone Boxes

Telephone boxes first came into use in England in the 1880s; at first they were installed in shops, post offices and railway stations, but by around 1900 boxes began to appear in the streets. It was not until the 1920s, however, after the Post Office had taken over the entire telephone system (except for Hull), that the first standard design began to appear. In 1921 the first kiosk, cast in concrete and glazed on two sides with a wooden door on either side, was introduced. On the roof were three enamelled boards with the word 'telephone' surmounted by scrolled ironwork. One still stands at Bembridge, Isle of Wight, and was scheduled in 1986 as a building of historic interest. In 1927 the first cast-iron box was produced to the design of Sir Giles Gilbert Scott, recognizable by the eighteen glass panels in each side surmounted by perforated crown ventilators. Scott also designed the 'Jubilee' box, which was introduced in 1936, becoming the first national standard design, and is still to be found in many of our villages.

Bibliography

I am indebted to numerous books and booklets, in particular the county and regional series published by Robert Hale and B.T. Batsford, which provided invaluable background information. The list which follows is by no means complete but includes those books that have proved most valuable.

Aaron, H., *Pillar to Post: Looking at Street Furniture* (Frederick Warne, 1982)

Addison, W., *English Fairs and Markets* (Batsford, 1953)

—— *Farmhouses in the English Landscape* (Hale, 1986)

Addy, S.O., *The Evolution of the English House* (Allen and Unwin, 1898)

Bailey, B., *Villages of England* (Weidenfeld and Nicolson, 1984)

—— *The English Village Green* (Hale, 1985)

Banks, F.J., *English Villages* (Batsford, 1963)

Barley, M.W., *The English Farmhouse and Cottage* (Routledge and Kegan Paul, 1976)

Barton, D.A., *Discovering Chapels and Meeting Houses* (Shire Publications, 1990)

Batsford, H. and Fry, C., *The English Cottage* (Batsford, 1938)

Bennett, J.D., *Discovering Monuments* (Shire Publications, 1969)

Bentley, J., *The Most Beautiful Villages of England* (Thames and Hudson, 1999)

Bland, J., *Odd and Unusual England* (Spur Books, 1970)

Blunden, E., *English Villages* (William Collins, 1942)

Bonham-Carter, V., *The English Village* (Penguin, 1951)

Brabbs, D., *English Country Churches* (Weidenfeld and Nicolson, 1986)

—— *English Country Pubs* (Phoenix Illustrated, 1997)

Briggs, M.S., *The English Farmhouse* (Batsford, 1953)

Brown, J. and Ward, S., *The Village Shop* (David and Charles, 1990)

Brunskill, A.W., *Illustrated Handbook of Vernacular Architecture* (Faber and Faber, 1971)

—— *Traditional Buildings of Britain* (Gollancz, 1981)

Burke, J., *The English Inn* (Batsford, 1981)

Burke, T., *The English Inn* (Jenkins, 1947)

Cave, L.F., *The Smaller English House – Its History and Development* (Hale, 1981)

Clifton-Taylor, A., *The Pattern of English Building* (Faber and Faber, 1972)

—— *The English Parish Church as Works of Art* (Batsford, 1974)

—— *Buildings of Delight* (Gollancz, 1988)

Cook, O. and Smith, E., *English Cottages and Farmhouses* (Thames and Hudson, 1954)

Crookston, P., *Village England* (Hutchinson, 1980)

Darley, G., *Villages of Vision* (Architectural Press, 1975)

Davies, P., *Troughs and Drinking Fountains* (Chatto and Windus, 1989)

Ditchfield, P.H., *The Charm of the English Village* (1908)

Eden, P., *Small Houses in England 1520–1820* (Historical Association, 1969)

Evans, T. and Lycett Green, C., *English Cottages* (Weidenfeld and Nicolson, 1982)

Filbee, M., *Cottage Industries* (David and Charles, 1982)

Friar, S., *The Batsford Companion to Local History* (Batsford, 1991)

Godfrey, W.H., *The English Almshouse* (Faber and Faber, 1955)

Greeves, L., *Country Cottages* (Pavilion Books, 1995)

Hadfield, J., *The Shell Book of English Villages* (Michael Joseph, 1980)

Hansell, P. and J., *Dovecotes* (Shire Publications, 1988)

—— *Doves and Dovecotes* (Millstream Books, 1988)

Hewett, C.A., *English Historic Carpentry* (Phillimore, 1980)

Hibbs, J., *The Country Chapel* (David and Charles, 1988)

Hogg, G., *The English Country Inn* (Batsford, 1981)

Hoskins, W.G., *The Making of the English Landscape* (Hodder and Stoughton, 1977)

Howard, F.E., *Medieval Styles of the Parish Church* (Batsford, 1936)

Howson, B., *Houses of Noble Poverty: A History of the English Almshouse* (Bellevue Books, 1993)

Johnson, D.E., *Essex Curiosities* (Spur Books, 1973)

Jones, S.R., *The Village Homes of England* (The Studio, 1912)

Laws, B., *Old English Farmhouses* (Collins and Brown, 1992)

Lea, R., *Country Curiosities* (Spur Books, 1973)

Lewis, J.R., *The Village School* (Hale, 1989)

Lindley, K., *Chapels and Meeting Houses* (Baker, 1969)

McKann, J., *Clay and Cob Buildings* (Shire Publications, 1983)

Mercer, E., *English Vernacular Houses* (Royal Commission on Historical Monuments, HMSO, 1975)

Moriarty, D., *Buildings of the Cotswolds* (Gollancz, 1989)

Mossman, K., *The Shell Book of Rural England* (David and Charles, 1969)

Muir, R., *The English Village* (Thames and Hudson, 1980)

—— *The Villages of England* (Thames and Hudson, 1992)

Nicholson G. and Fawcett, J., *The Village in England* (Rizzoli International Publications, 1988)

Pakington, H., *English Villages and Hamlets* (Batsford, 1934)

Paulin, K. and Bruning, T., *The David and Charles Book of Historic English Inns* (David and Charles, 1982)

Penoyre J. and J., *Houses in the Landscape* (Faber and Faber, 1978)

Perry, C., Gore, A. and Fleming, L., *Old English Villages* (Weidenfeld and Nicolson, 1986)

Peters, J.E.C., *Discovering Traditional Farm Buildings* (Shire Publications, 1981)

Pevsner, N., *The Buildings of England* series (Penguin, various dates)

Powell, C., *Discovering Cottage Architecture* (Shire Publications, 1987)

Prizeman, J., *Your House – The Outside View* (Hutchinson, 1975)

Quiney, A., *The Traditional Buildings of England* (Thames and Hudson, 1990)

Quiney, A. and Meers, N., *Panoramas of English Villages* (Phoenix Illustrated, 1997)

Randall, G., *The English Parish Church* (Batsford, 1982)

Reid, R., *The Shell Book of Cottages* (Michael Joseph, 1977)

Reynolds, J., *Windmills and Watermills* (Hugh Evelyn, 1970)

Roberts, B.K., *The Making of the English Village* (Longman, 1987)

—— *Village Plans* (Shire Publications, 1982)

Rowley, T., *Villages in the Landscape* (Dent, 1978)

Sisson, M., *Country Cottages* (Methuen, 1949)

Talbot, R. and Whiteman, R., *England* (Cassell and Co., 2000)

—— *Cotswold Landscapes* (Weidenfeld and Nicolson, 1999)

Timpson, J., *Timpson's England* (Jarrold, 1987)

—— *Timpson's Other England* (Jarrold, 1993)

Turpin, R. and Hunt, R., *Villages of England* (Harper Collins, 1999)

Vince, J.N.T., *Discovering Windmills* (Shire Publications, 1969)

—— *Discovering Watermills* (Shire Publications, 1987)

Wailes, R., *The English Windmill* (Routledge and Kegan Paul, 1954)

Warren, C.H., *English Cottages and Farmhouses* (Collins, 1948)

Warren, G., *Vanishing Street Furniture* (David and Charles, 1978)

Wenham, P., *Watermills* (Hale, 1989)

Wright, G., *Stone Villages of Britain* (David and Charles, 1985)

Place Index

Page numbers in italics refer to illustrations

General Index